Jiddu Krishnamurti was born in south India in 1895. In 1911, at the age of fifteen, he and his brother Nitya were brought by Annie Besant to England to be educated. Krishnamurti had been proclaimed to be the coming World Teacher by Theosophists, who set up a large organization around him, but in 1929, saying he did not want followers, he dissolved it, and returned lands and monies that had been donated for it. He then travelled almost ceaselessly for over sixty years through most parts of the world giving public talks and private interviews. The essence of his teaching is that only a complete change of consciousness in people can bring about a change in society and so peace in the world. He taught that this change could take place in every person, not gradually but instantaneously. It is only in seeing ourselves as we are with absolute clarity that real revolution, which must be inner, takes place. Krishnamurti died in 1986.

Beginnings of Learning

KRISHNAMURTI

PHOENIX

A PHOENIX PAPERBACK

First published in Great Britain in 1975
by Victor Gollancz Ltd
First published in paperback in 1978
by Penguin Books
Reprinted in 1990
by Arkana
This paperback edition published in 2003
by Phoenix,
an imprint of Orion Books Ltd,
Orion House, 5 Upper St Martin's Lane,
London WC2H 9EA

ISBN 0 75381 687 3

Printed and bound in Great Britain by
Clays Ltd, St Ives plc

CONTENTS

PART ONE

Conversations with Students and Staff at Brockwood Park

Contents

PART TWO

Conversations with Parents and Teachers

Page 215

PART I: QUOTATIONS

The world is that way, deceptive, the deceiving politicians, the money-minded ... If you are not properly educated you'll just slip into it. So what do you think is education? Is it to help you fit into the mechanism of the present order, or disorder, of things? Or do you think it should be something else?

Is your education at Brockwood helping you to be intelligent? I mean by that word to be very sensitive, not to your own desires, to your own demands, but to be sensitive to the world, to what is going on in the world. Surely education is not merely to give you knowledge, but also to give you the capacity to look at the world objectively. The function of education is to help you to face the world in a totally different intelligent way.

When you have that seed, and it is flowering here, then you will keep it going all your life. But if this doesn't operate, then the world will destroy you. The world makes you what it wants you to be: a cunning animal.

PART ONE

*Conversations with Students and Staff at
Brockwood Park*

I

Problems of living at Brockwood where there is no authority. Difference between sentiment and affection. The feeling of being 'at home'.

KRISHNAMURTI: Most people work either to avoid punishment or to gain something in the way of possessions, money, fame and so on. So most people work under great pressure. Here at Brockwood there is not that extreme pressure, or any kind of pressure put upon you. Therefore there is a tendency, if I may point out, to slacken, to let go, to become rather empty and lose that vitality that youth generally has – that feeling of urgency, the flame of doing something. All that gradually disappears and you are left here to be responsible to yourself, which is rather difficult.

Most of us want somebody to lean on, somebody to encourage us, somebody to say, 'You are doing very well, carry on!' And to push us a little when we are slack, drive us when we are indifferent, when we are sleepy, shake us to keep awake so that somebody gradually becomes the authority. Haven't you noticed this?

There is no authority here, therefore you are left to yourself and it is very difficult to keep oneself at the highest point of energy, drive, intelligence and affection and not just go off into a kind of day-dream, uselessly wasting time. Brockwood is supposed to give you – and I hope it does – the terrain, the environment, the atmosphere in which this self-generating energy can go on. How is all this to be created? Who is going to do it?

Questioner: Everyone here.

KRISHNAMURTI: What does that mean?

13

Questioner: Self-responsibility.

KRISHNAMURTI: When you use a word be very careful that you know what it means. Do you know what that word 'responsibility' means? – not what you think it should mean, but what it means according to the dictionary. We must first understand the meaning of that word. Here is your English teacher, ask her.

Questioner: Doesn't it mean the ability to respond?

KRISHNAMURTI: That's right, isn't it? – the capacity to respond.

Questioner: We often use the word 'answerable'; we say, 'I am answerable for such and such.'

KRISHNAMURTI: If I am inefficient I can't answer, respond properly. So responsibility means to respond adequately to the job or to the environment or to the incidents around me. I must respond to my highest capacity: that is what the word 'responsible' means. See what a lot is involved in that one word.

So who is going to be responsible to bring about the right soil here, the right environment, the right atmosphere, so that you are totally awake, generating the energy for yourself?

Questioner: Each one of us.

KRISHNAMURTI: Can you do this, Gregory? Is each one of us capable of this?

Questioner: All of us together.

KRISHNAMURTI: No. Who is 'All of us together'? Will *you* be responsible to bring about this soil where you will respond to an incident, to everything that is happening around you completely, adequately? If each one of us does that there is no problem, is there? Then the place will be marvellous and each one of us will have a thousand-watt candle inside him. Is each one of us capable of this? That is, when you say, 'I'll go to bed at ten o'clock' – or whatever you agree on – you will do it and nobody need tell you. You follow what it implies? When you study you give your complete attention to it, that means an adequate response to the subject, to everything which is your responsibility. Can we all do this together?

Questioner: We are capable of it, but we don't usually do it.

KRISHNAMURTI: Why not? Are you slack or indifferent to what you are doing because you want to be doing something else?

Questioner: First, how can one be responsible if one doesn't know the field in which one is working well enough. I mean, before I can take responsibility for something, I have to know for certain that I can do it.

KRISHNAMURTI: Yes, that you are capable of doing it.

Questioner: But mostly what happens is that people are saying, ' You are responsible,' and it's taken for granted that one knows what to do.

KRISHNAMURTI: No, look, Tungki, we have just now defined that word. I am asking you, are you capable, adequate, sufficiently intelligent to deal with something that has to take place here? If we are not, let's be humble about it, let's be sensible and say: we are not. Then how do we bring this about in us? Discuss it, I am not going to answer for you.

Questioner: It has something to do with relationship. When you are responsible, you are responsible in relationship, aren't you?

KRISHNAMURTI: I don't know – find out.

Questioner: I see so many misunderstandings in the school, very often among the students, among the staff. But I realize now that in order to be responsible we have to see first that we have misunderstandings which must be cleared up.

KRISHNAMURTI: Now how do you clear up a misunderstanding? What is the requisite quality necessary to help us to wipe away a misunderstanding? You say something and I misunderstand it and I get hurt. How do you and I wipe away that hurt, that sense of 'You've misunderstood me'? Or I have done something out of misunderstanding which you think I ought not to have done. How do you clear that up?

Questioner: You go back to the beginning and see what went wrong.

KRISHNAMURTI: Is it necessary to do all that?

Questioner: It needs time.

KRISHNAMURTI: No, it needs a little more than that – what else is necessary?

Questioner: A regard, a proper relationship.

KRISHNAMURTI: Which means what? Go on, push.

Questioner: (1) It needs patience and care, a feeling of eagerness.

Questioner: (2) I would say affection.

KRISHNAMURTI: Peter says it needs affection – you understand? If I have affection I say, 'Let's look at the misunderstanding and see if we can't get over it.' But if I merely examine it intellectually and take time over it, then I'll be hurt by somebody else. So affection is the basis on which one can wipe away misunderstandings. Right?

Questioner: I think if you didn't have an image about yourself you wouldn't be hurt.

KRISHNAMURTI: Yes, but I have an image and he has an image. I get hurt by what you have said; how do I wipe it away? Can I say, 'Look, I have misunderstood, I am sorry, do let us talk about it again'? That requires a certain affection, doesn't it? Have you got that affection? Affection is different from sentiment – be very clear on that point.

16

Questioner: What does sentiment mean?

KRISHNAMURTI: Feeling.

Questioner: But it's not right feeling.

KRISHNAMURTI: Now find out the difference between affection, love and sentiment. We said sentiment is feeling, emotionalism. 'I feel I should do this, I feel I am a great man, I feel anger' – that is a sentiment. 'I love children': in that there is a great deal of sentiment because I don't want to do things which may hurt them. Sentiment implies a feeling. Now what is affection and what is sentiment?

Questioner: Somehow there is a self-deceptive element in sentiment.

KRISHNAMURTI: Yes, that's right. Sentiment can become hard: sentiment can become efficient but cruel.

Questioner: You often find a sentimental person is capable of being brutal in another mood. Like the Nazis, who were sentimental about music and the arts, but very brutal.

KRISHNAMURTI: That's right. But we have all got that feeling in us also, so don't let us put it on certain types of people. That is, we can be sentimental, go into a kind of ecstatic nothingness over music, over painting, we can say, 'I love Nature', and the next minute hit someone on the head because he thwarts us. So sentiment is one thing and affection is another. If I have affection for you I am going to talk things over with you. I say, 'Don't be rough, be quiet, sit down, talk to me, I have misunderstood you. I want to talk it over with you because I have affection for you.' I have no sentiment for you but I have affection for you. I don't know whether you see the difference – do you?

Questioner: I think younger people often feel that sentiment is something sloppy.

KRISHNAMURTI: I agree.

17

Questioner: Because if you have a sentiment it becomes mechanical, you automatically have a reaction.

KRISHNAMURTI: You see, idealism is sentimentality and therefore it breeds hypocrisy – I do not know whether you see that.

Questioner: Because it has moods.

KRISHNAMURTI: That's right, all that is involved in sentiment. That being clear, have we this affection so that when there is a misunderstanding we can talk about it and get it over, not store it up?

Questioner: Perhaps the word 'sentimentality' needs a definition. I mean, it seems to go even further than sentiment. It's a second-hand emotion.

KRISHNAMURTI: It's an ugly thing.

Questioner: It's mostly put on.

KRISHNAMURTI: Yes, that's right, like a mask you put on.

Questioner: It seems that it is difficult to distinguish in daily life. Let's take an example: I see a beautiful tree. What is that feeling?

KRISHNAMURTI: Is that sentiment? I look at that tree and say, 'What a marvellous tree that is, how beautiful,' – is that sentiment?

Questioner: Sir, are you talking to yourself when you say that?

KRISHNAMURTI: Yes. I say, 'How beautiful that is' to myself. You may be there and then I would say, 'Look, how lovely that tree is.' Is that sentiment?

Questioner: It's a fact. But when you see a tree and think you ought to feel it is beautiful that is a sentiment.

KRISHNAMURTI: Yes, that's it – you've understood? Have you absorbed it?

Questioner: Yes. Which is, when you think you ought to . . .

KRISHNAMURTI: That's right. So when I feel sentimental about something I put on a false front: I 'ought' to feel that is a beautiful tree.

Questioner: It's an act of behaviour.

KRISHNAMURTI: Yes, an act of behaviour. I am glad we are getting into this.

Questioner: Yes, but now, continuing your story, you take care of that tree and become attached. Then does sentimentality come in?

KRISHNAMURTI: Yes. When you become attached, sentimentality creeps in. So absorb it, it's a food you are chewing – you have to digest it. You ask: when there is affection, is there attachment?

Questioner: No, but sometimes one jumps to the other without realizing it.

KRISHNAMURTI: Of course.

Questioner: There seems to be no boundary.

KRISHNAMURTI: So you have to go very slowly. We are trying to differentiate between affection and sentimentality. We see what sentimentality is. Most of us don't feel sentimental when we are young, but as we grow older we put on many unnecessary masks and say, 'We must feel the beauty of that tree.' Or, 'I must love that poem because Keats or Shelley wrote it.' Affection is something entirely different. Sentimentality is affectation, hypocrisy. Now, what is affection?

Questioner: It literally means to move towards somebody.

KRISHNAMURTI: Yes, doesn't it?

Questioner: To be affected by something.

KRISHNAMURTI: First listen to what Mr Simmons said.

We have to listen to each other. He said: 'To move towards somebody.' That means what?

Questioner: You feel for them.

KRISHNAMURTI: Be careful – don't say 'feel'. I move towards you, you may be rigid but I move towards you, I make a gesture towards you. I stretch out my hand to you, you may not want it but I stretch it out. Affection means, 'to move towards' – the tree, the bird, the lake, or a human being – to stretch out your arm, your hand, to make a gesture, smile; all that is affection, isn't it? If I stretch my hand out to you though I've misunderstood you, you immediately say, 'Yes, I'll try and wipe it out.' Unless there is a movement towards you the misunderstanding cannot be got rid of.

Questioner: But some people might just stretch out their hand mechanically.

KRISHNAMURTI: That is sentimentality, that is hypocrisy.

Questioner: And if you are affected by somebody, that can be a form of getting worked up in the same way.

KRISHNAMURTI: That's right.

Questioner: We soon have to leave Brockwood, and then we meet people who are sentimental: our mother, or some person like that. You have to respond to her sentiments.

KRISHNAMURTI: I know. You see, then love is not sentiment or sentimentality. Love is something very hard, if I can use that word. You understand what it means? Not hard in the sense of brutal, it has no hypocrisy, no sentimentality, it has no clothing around it.

Questioner: Down to earth, you mean?

KRISHNAMURTI: If you like to put it that way.

We know now what we mean by affection, love and sentimentality. How do we create the environment here, the terrain, the soil in which there is that sense of freedom from pressure and hence non-dependence, so that you yourself generate this tremendous feeling of living, of vitality, of flame – whatever you like to call it. How do we set about it? It's your responsibility. Do you now understand the meaning of that word? What will you do to bring about this atmosphere? – because each one of us is responsible. It's not Mr or Mrs Simmons or X, Y, Z – *you* are responsible.

Questioner: Surely affection cannot be cultivated?

KRISHNAMURTI: Then what will you do? We said affection is necessary, but we are asking how do you create this atmosphere in which affection can function?

Questioner: If we can see it when we occasionally have this affection, then we can see the situation which encourages us to have it.

KRISHNAMURTI: You are not answering the question. Here at Brockwood we are responsible for creating this soil in which there is freedom, which is non-dependency. In that freedom, in this energy we can flower in goodness. How are we to create that?

Questioner: Perhaps we could meet Tungki's point there, because I think some of us have felt the same thing. What he said was, we have felt moments of affection in the past and if we can analyse that, perhaps we can see what brought it about. If that's a false trail, perhaps we can finish with it. We know we have felt affection, it has happened.

KRISHNAMURTI: Why does it disappear? Can it? Or was it sentimentality and therefore it has gone? You say, 'I've felt sometimes, or often, this sense of great affection, but somehow it goes and comes back occasionally.' Now, can affection go away or is it sentimentality that can wither?

Questioner: We feel affection and in trying to hold on to it and perpetuate it we become sentimental, because we try to recognize its symptoms and what it does, and we act according to memory.

KRISHNAMURTI: Or it may be sentimentality, which we call affection.

Questioner: Yes, if it's real affection I don't see how it can dissolve.

KRISHNAMURTI: That's right.

Questioner: It gets buried maybe, but it doesn't dissolve. It can be buried by misunderstandings and it can re-emerge.

KRISHNAMURTI: Can it? If I have real affection can you bury it? No. Most of us haven't got this great sense of affection. Now how do we bring it about? Don't say 'cultivate it', that takes time.

Questioner: Isn't it part of seeing the necessity? During the first talks you had with us you tried to show us the necessity of this place.

KRISHNAMURTI: Look, affection can't be cultivated, can it? To say, 'I love you' that feeling must come naturally, not be forced or stimulated. One can't say, 'It is necessary therefore I must love you.' How do you have this affection? Can you take time over it? Find out. It may be that you must come to it obliquely – you understand what I mean?

Questioner: Perhaps you have to find out what stops you from having affection.

KRISHNAMURTI: But you must have it before you can find out what stops it. Anger, jealousy, misunderstanding – will all those things stop affection?

Questioner: Yes.

KRISHNAMURTI: Will they? You say something brutal – will that destroy my affection? I am hurt, but the real thing, the beauty of affection, will that be destroyed? So it may be that we can come upon it from a different direction. Shall we investigate that possibility? I am full of sentimentality, emotionalism, idealism, of 'This should be done', 'That must be done', 'I will try'. Those are all sentimentalities.

We said affection is a very hard reality, it's a fact, you can't distort it, you can't destroy it. If I haven't got it I want to find out how I am to come upon it. I can't cultivate it, I can't nourish it by good deeds, saying, 'I must go and help you when you are sick'; that is not affection. There must be a way of doing something that will bring it about. We'll find out. What do you think?

Questioner: If I've never experienced it, how can I know that it is there?

KRISHNAMURTI: I am going to find out, I don't know, I haven't got any affection. I may have it occasionally when I am half-asleep, but actually I haven't got it when I am living, struggling. Now how is that seed to flower in me?

Questioner: You have to lose your images of people.

KRISHNAMURTI: That's one thing. I want to come much nearer.

Questioner: Also, there are many things that are preventing it, maybe we can look at those things.

KRISHNAMURTI: Yes, go on. But will that do it?

Questioner: I can't do it before I've looked at what is preventing me.

KRISHNAMURTI: Maybe I am angry, I get easily irritated and misunderstood. So I say: let me wipe it out. Will affection come? I know many people, so-called monks, good social workers and so on, who have trained themselves not to be angry. But the real flame has gone, they never had it, they are kind, generous people, they will help you, will give you their money, their coat, their shelter, but the real thing is nowhere there. I want to find out how to let this thing flower in us; once it flowers you can't destroy it.

You have said: see the things that prevent it. That means you are deliberately cultivating affection. When you say, 'I will see what the things are which are blocking me', that is a

deliberate act in order to get it. I don't know whether you
see this.

Questioner: Yes.

KRISHNAMURTI: Therefore you are trying to cultivate it,
aren't you? – only in an obscure way.

*Questioner: (1) You said that we must try to find the soil for affec-
tion, for this sense of responsibility.*

*Questioner: (2) If we try to create a certain relationship, an atmos-
phere, whatever you call it, in which this can flower, isn't that perhaps what she meant?*

KRISHNAMURTI: I am trying to point out that you cannot
cultivate it.

Questioner: But can you not bring about the right 'something'?

KRISHNAMURTI: That's what I'm trying to find out. So
let's forget affection as you cannot cultivate it. I wonder if
you understand this? You can cultivate chrysanthemums or
other things, but you cannot cultivate affection – cunningly,
unconsciously or deliberately, you can't produce this. So
what are we to do?

*Questioner: It seems to me that there is something – not to do – but
that you can recognize. When you are looking at somebody, or a
situation, and you recognize there is no affection, that takes no time.*

KRISHNAMURTI: That can be done. What takes place
when you say, 'Yes. I see when I look at you that I really
have no affection for you.' What has happened?

Questioner: You have faced a fact. Something happens.

KRISHNAMURTI: Does it? Listen: unconsciously, deeply,
this idea that there must be affection exists. I do various
things in order to capture it. And it cannot be captured.
You are all suggesting methods to capture it.

*Questioner: I was not suggesting a method, I was only saying:
recognize that you haven't got it.*

KRISHNAMURTI: Yes, I haven't got it, I know that very well. That flame isn't there.

Questioner: It's quite hard to really see that it's not there, we go on pretending.

KRISHNAMURTI: I like to look at things as they are and face facts; personally I have no sentimentality of any kind in me, I strip away all that. Now I say, 'I do not have this thing.' And also I know it cannot be cultivated surreptitiously in a round-about way. Yet I vaguely see the beauty of it. So what am I to do? May we move away from that and come back to it a little later?

KRISHNAMURTI: Just listen to what I have to say. Do you feel at home here? Do you know what a home is?

Questioner: The place where you know you always get support and help. You feel comfortable, you don't feel self-conscious, you move more easily at home than where you are a stranger.

KRISHNAMURTI: At home you are not a stranger. Is that it?

Questioner: (1) In that case you have many homes, because you may have many friends and brothers. I can feel comfortable in many places.

Questioner: (2) You can have a house and live in it, but that doesn't mean it's a home.

KRISHNAMURTI: What makes it a home?

Questioner: (1) To have affection and co-operation between the people who are living there.

Questioner: (2) A home is a place where you have security.

KRISHNAMURTI: Is that what you call a home? – where you have security, where you feel comfortable, where you are not a stranger?

25

Questioner: It's all these things.

KRISHNAMURTI: Tell me more.

Questioner: (1) Where you have no fear.

Questioner: (2) Actually I don't consider I have a 'home'; I have a house in California, I go to school here.

KRISHNAMURTI: He said something just then which was slurred over unfortunately. He said, 'Friends and brothers', and also, 'Wherever I am I'm at home'. You said that – don't withdraw it! Now what is a home to you all? You said, wherever I am I feel at home. Where I am not a stranger, where I am comfortable, where I am not treated as an outsider, where I can do anything I want to without getting scolded – is that a home? They *do* scold you, they make you go to bed at a certain time. So what is a home?

Questioner: A feeling in yourself about being at home?

KRISHNAMURTI: What is that feeling? Sentimentality? You must be careful here. Please pay attention, I am going to push you into this. I want to find out what is a home to you, actually, not theoretically. I go all over the world – except to Russia and China – I am put into different rooms, small rooms or big rooms. I have slept on the floor, I have slept on silver beds, I have slept in all kinds of places, and I have felt at home – you understand? To me, home means wherever I am. Sometimes there is a plain wall in front of my window, sometimes there is a beautiful garden, sometimes there is a slum next door – I am telling you accurate things, not just something imaginary. Sometimes there is a tremendous noise going on around me, the floor is dirty and so on – the mattresses I've slept on! I am at home as I am at home here. It means I bring my own home – you understand?

Is Brockwood a home to you? In the sense of a place where you can talk to each other, feel happy, play, climb a tree when you want to, where there is no scolding, no punishment, no pressure, where you feel completely protected, feel that somebody is looking after you, taking trouble to see that you are clean, that your clothes are clean, that you comb your hair? Where you feel that you are completely secure and free? That's a home, isn't it?

Questioner: What brings that about is self-responsibility, so that someone else doesn't have to push you into doing things.

KRISHNAMURTI: No, don't go on to something else. Is this a home to you in that sense?

Questioner: Yes.

KRISHNAMURTI: Are you sure that you feel you are safe, protected, watched over, cared for, never blamed, being told affectionately not to do certain things?

Questioner: Do we ever feel safe, wherever we are?

KRISHNAMURTI: Oh, don't theorize. I am asking you, Tungki, if you feel at home here, in the sense which we all agreed is more or less a home. Do you feel that?

Questioner: Yes, more or less.

KRISHNAMURTI: When I said more or less, it was in the sense that I can add more to it – whether there are good books, good food, whether it is in good taste, where nobody scolds you. Do you understand what I mean?

Questioner: I think it is such an 'ideal' place that nobody dares say that we do scold.

KRISHNAMURTI: Ideals are sentimentality.

Questioner: Yes, but we do scold.

KRISHNAMURTI: Scold affectionately, that's understood. Now is this a home to you? Don't be casual.

Questioner: One does feel cared for here.

KRISHNAMURTI: So please tell me if you feel at home –
I'm not saying you do or don't, it's up to you to tell me. If
you don't want to tell me, that's all right too. If you feel at
home here, are you also responsible?

Questioner: If I'm not, I won't feel at home.

KRISHNAMURTI: That's why I am asking. I carry a piece
of furniture from this room to the next and I bang it and I
don't care. If it's my home I am going to take care – you
follow?

So that is what I mean by responsive, responsible. When
you feel at home you look after things, you look after yourself, you don't want to hurt your mother, make too much
work for her. It's a kind of mutual, affectionate, creative
movement. Don't you know all these things? The moment
you feel at home, what takes place?

Questioner: Affection.

KRISHNAMURTI: Affection, isn't it? Then you can say to
me: for goodness' sake don't break up that furniture; and
because I feel at home I won't get hurt. I wonder if you
understand what I am talking about? So where you are at
home the seed begins to germinate, you don't have to cultivate it, it begins to flower. Is that what is happening with all
of you? If you don't feel at home here find out whose fault
it is, whether it is yours or somebody else's; correct it, don't
sit back and say, 'Well, I don't feel at home' – do something about it. When you grow up you will leave this place
and you will have to face the world. And if you haven't this
seed in you here, the world is going to destroy you. They
will trample on you, they are wolves, murderers – don't
mistake it. This feeling that you are completely relaxed,
completely at home – in the sense I am using that word –
that brings about the responsibility which is affectionate.
Do you understand this? Please do. And when you have
that seed and it is flowering here, then you will keep it
going all your life. But if it doesn't operate, then the world

will destroy you; the world makes you what it wants you to be: a cunning animal.

So let's find out if you are at home here and if you aren't, why not? Affection is non-dependency, I don't know if you realize this. Some of you are going to get married; you will say to your wife, 'I love you, darling.' Then you go off to the office or to some other kind of work, and there you are full of anxiety, wanting to further yourself, full of ambition, greedy. Back home you say, 'Darling, I love you.' You see the absurdity of it? That's what is going on in the world. In that there is attachment, jealousy, fear, anxiety: she mustn't look at anybody else except me.

If parents really cared for their children there would be no wars. They would say, 'Live, don't kill, live.' There would be no army – see what would happen. So what is generally called home is not a home at all. Therefore *this* must be your home; you spend eight or nine months of the year here and it's your responsibility – we know what that means – to make it your home, to tell me, or Mrs Simmons or whoever, 'This is not my home because you're not doing certain things' – you follow? Then you share in this. Are you just listening, or are you taking part? Apply yourself, create, don't let everybody else do all the work and say, 'Yes, I am very comfortable here, this is my home.' Then it's not your home, because you haven't built it.

You see, from an early age I have been living in other people's houses and I have never had a place of which I could say, 'This is my home.' But there is the feeling that you are at home wherever you are because you are responsible, you are affectionate. Home is not a creation of sentimentality, it is a creation of fact – the fact that I feel at home. That is, I am free, I am responsible, I am affectionate. Total responsibility is the feeling of being at home.

2

State of the world. Need to educate ourselves. Implications of learning. Learning about co-operation. Many and varied activities. Skill in action: Yoga.

KRISHNAMURTI: Do you know what is happening in the world? – the hi-jacking, the deception, outright lying, re-volt, and the chaos and the misery in India. When you read about it, what does it mean to you? Or don't you read about it – are you not aware of what is happening?

Questioner: A lot of it is very sad.

KRISHNAMURTI: What do you mean by that word?

Questioner: Some people are dominating others and hurting lots of people.

KRISHNAMURTI: But that has been going on for centuries, hasn't it? – all history is that. What do you think of it?

Questioner: It doesn't really affect me.

KRISHNAMURTI: Why do you say it doesn't affect you?

Questioner: I see people getting killed on television. I look at it and I don't realize that those are people getting killed.

KRISHNAMURTI: What part do you play in all that?

Questioner: I'm not part of it.

KRISHNAMURTI: Then what is your relationship to it? Is it something that is happening 'over there', in Jordan, in America?

Questioner: Sometimes it hits home and I can feel what those people are feeling.

KRISHNAMURTI: Do you feel that one must change all this, or that you can't do anything about it? What is your relationship to the world? Is it an awareness of the extraordinary things that are going on technologically and the appalling inefficiency of man to meet that technological advance? What is your relationship to the confusion that man is producing all round the world?

Questioner: As long as we are confused we are contributing to the confusion.

KRISHNAMURTI: I understand that, but what do you feel about it? What is your innermost response to all this?

Questioner: I feel frustrated and angry that all this is happening. I have reactions to it; I see things which are wrong and I get hostile.

KRISHNAMURTI: And then what? You see, when you leave here, go on to university or through college, what part are you going to play in it all? Will you just fit into the machinery of it? What's going to become of you in relation to the world? Or are you not interested in that at present? You may say, 'I'm too young to consider all this, I'll have a good time and enjoy life while I can; later on I will think about it.' Or do you feel that this is a preparation, a commencement of what it is going to be when you grow older? One can revolt now and take drugs – or not, this or that – but when you are twenty or twenty-five you will get married. Will you fit into all this? If you don't fit in, what are you going to do? If you are antagonistic to the system, to what is happening – not hypocritical but actually in revolt – can you pretend that you don't really feel the appallingness of all this? What is your response?

Don't you consider what you are going to be at all? Get married and settle down? – if that is the end result, then what is education? Is it to help you to get settled down in life in this system? I have heard many students in India, when asked, 'What are you going to do?' reply, 'Oh, Sir, my father wants me to be an engineer, my father wishes me to be a doctor, we need doctors. I want to help India through becoming an efficient engineer.' The majority of them think in terms of a professional career, they want to help the backward country, do social work. Is that what you are all going to do? Are you all asleep?

I think that's where the sadness lies, not in what the world is. The world is that way, deceptive, the deceiving politicians, the money-minded – all that. If you are not properly educated you'll just slip into it. So what do you think is education? Is it to help you to fit into the mechanism of the present order, or disorder, of things or do you think it should be something else? If it is something else, what is it that you want?

Questioner: It's just a learning process.

KRISHNAMURTI: What do you mean by learning?

Questioner: Finding out about things around you and in you.

KRISHNAMURTI: Are you doing it?

Questioner: Yes.

KRISHNAMURTI: Do you really want to learn?

Questioner: Yes, I do.

KRISHNAMURTI: Be terribly serious – don't let's talk easily, glibly. Do you know what it means to learn?

Questioner: To find out as much as one can about whatever it is – about everything.

KRISHNAMURTI: Is that what you mean by 'learn'? – to find out? You can pick up an encyclopaedia; you can find out everything there.

Questioner: That only encompasses the theoretical side.

KRISHNAMURTI: Then what do you mean by learning?

Questioner: Finding out something and being able to deal with it, cope with it, and possibly even use it.

32

KRISHNAMURTI: We were talking the other day about co-operation, intelligence and sex.* We discussed in principle what co-operation is, what it means to co-operate, to work together, to do things together. How are you going to learn about it – is it just a theory? A small community is living here at Brockwood. Any civilized man – civilized in the sense of cultured, thoughtful, intelligent – must co-operate, life demands co-operation – not with what you like, but the spirit of co-operation. You said, 'I want to learn about co-operation.' Now how do you learn about it? Because in any cultured society there must be co-operation; it can't exist otherwise. How are you going to learn about it?

Questioner: In discussing it. There is some learning involved in that.

KRISHNAMURTI: I am asking what do you mean by learning about co-operation? We both agree, life cannot go on if there is no co-operation. Where do I begin?

Questioner: By co-operating.

KRISHNAMURTI: What do you mean by that word co-operation, how do you co-operate, with whom, why? Where do I learn it?

Questioner: By doing it.

KRISHNAMURTI: What do you mean by doing it – investigate, learn.

Questioner: Find out why you want to co-operate.

KRISHNAMURTI: So are you going to learn? Is the process of learning asking this question? And also, do you have the spirit of co-operation, the feeling? Do you really, deeply want to co-operate? Don't you have to begin there? – to learn whether you really, deep down, want to co-operate. Because if you don't know what it means, you will never know what it means *not* to co-operate. If the State says, 'Go

*See Chapter 5.

33

and kill,' unless you know what co-operation is, how do you know when not to co-operate?

Now tell me, please, how are you going to find out for yourself whether you have the spirit of co-operation – not with me, or about something – but the feeling of it. Isn't that the beginning of learning about co-operation? Where do you begin to learn – from a book? If you say, 'Learning begins with a book', then you have the encyclopaedias, a vast knowledge accumulated in pages or in the brain of a teacher, but is that where you begin to learn? For instance, either I believe in an idea, and therefore I want you and others to co-operate with me in carrying out that idea, which is generally called co-operation; because we both believe in that idea, in a principle, in a system. Or, we have the feeling of co-operation – not about what and with whom, but the *feeling*. Do you deeply understand the meaning of that word? I mean not only working together but feeling together that certain things must be done – the feeling first, and the action.

When you say you want to learn in a community, in a school like this, there is a problem. There are older people and the younger generation, the teacher and the students and others coming here; there must be a way to live happily, intelligently, actively, with a great deal of energy. One must have this feeling, otherwise we'll all pull in different directions. So I want to learn and my first enquiry in learning is to find out if I really want to co-operate, if I really have the feeling of it. Have you? If you don't have it find out why. This extraordinary quality, this feeling for co-operation, building together, doing things together, this is what has built this world.

Questioner: What do you mean by ' It has built this world'?

KRISHNAMURTI: The world, in the sense of the railway, the post office, sending a rocket to the moon – three hundred thousand men were involved in that and had to co-operate; they co-operated for patriotic or financial reasons, reasons of vanity and so on. There, they co-operated round an idea in which was involved prestige, competition with Russia and so on. Now can there be real, deep, lasting co-operation when there is a motive? If I have any form of selfish regard, a self-interested motive, can there be co-operation in the sense we want to understand it?

Questioner: You want to get something out of it, you don't have to do it.

KRISHNAMURTI: Therefore find out if you have got the feeling of getting something out of it. You are beginning to learn something which you can't learn from a book.

Questioner: The idea of getting something out of it doesn't necessarily come in. If we want to build a house, I see that it will be easier for you and me to work along together. We organize it from the start and we co-operate with one another to build the house. Therefore I have the idea of building a house; we are going to get a house out of it, you and I.

KRISHNAMURTI: Quite – go further. You can go a little deeper.

Questioner: So what happens when you want a white house and I don't.

KRISHNAMURTI: That's it. You want a square room and she wants a long room. You think you know much better than she does. Look what you are doing. Dominic said just now that we will co-operate if we want to build a house together, because he is going to get a house out of it. But if we begin to disagree on what kind of rooms it's going to have, we'll fall out. So what does that mean?

Questioner: If you start with the spirit of co-operation and you both want to build something together, won't you still have a problem?

KRISHNAMURTI: You'll still have the problem – how will you tackle it? You and I want to co-operate, we want to build a house, you want a square room and I want a long one. And yet we both have the spirit of co-operation. What shall we do?

Questioner: We try to find out why you want a long room and why I want a square one.

KRISHNAMURTI: Which means what?

Questioner: We co-operate.

KRISHNAMURTI: Which means we are both willing to yield. You don't stick to your point, I don't stick to mine. Which means what?

Questioner: You don't have a fixed idea, so you are learning.

KRISHNAMURTI: It means you have a pliable mind, you don't say, 'I must have it', you are willing to change, which means you are not holding on to your particular desire, to your particular opinion.

Questioner: Say you are willing to think about it and the other person isn't.

KRISHNAMURTI: What will you do?

Questioner: I guess you would do what the other person wants – if you are willing to discuss and they are not.

KRISHNAMURTI: That's just it, what do you do if you want to co-operate and another doesn't?

Questioner: See the point of that person.

KRISHNAMURTI: But in a community like this, what are you to do?

Questioner: (1) You have to talk it over with them until they are back to co-operating. You see, I would be the one who would be yielding – I'm looking at it from my point of view – I'd be willing to talk about it. I don't know what I would do if the other person didn't want to.

Questioner: (2) *Perhaps instead of talking about the room you would start talking about co-operation itself, because this is the cause of the problem.*

Questioner: (3) *And you have to have the spirit of co-operation to begin with.*

KRISHNAMURTI: But I haven't got it. Take a wider issue. Generally we worship the intellect, the clever person who passes exams brilliantly is the most respected. Intellectually he is sharp, alive, good at his subject; playing games and doing anything in the garden is a bore to him. See how important it is that we should not only have a good brain, but also that we should be able to do things – to garden, cook, wash up – not just be one-sided. Intelligence implies being able to do things, not to say, 'I don't like gardening, it bores me, I only like to study.' That is a lop-sided way of living.

Now I'm going to propose that here we should not only have really first-class brains, that is to be able to think logically, sanely, dispassionately, not personally. But also one must have skill in action. You know Yoga? – that word also means 'skill in action', not just doing a few exercises. How are you going to have that skill in action?

Questioner: Through practice.

KRISHNAMURTI: Which means *doing* things. I would like to suggest – I have done a great deal of it in my life – that everyone should do some kind of work with the earth: gardening, planting, tending it – not just say, 'I'll plant, you'll go and water.' Looking after it, caring for it – that gives you an opportunity to care for something. Have you ever dug the soil? – you get in touch with the earth. I am going to propose that there should be not only an intellectual activity of the highest order here, but also a great deal of intense, active, clear thinking, working, studying at the highest level. And also to have skill in action, which is doing things. When you play the guitar, play it properly, not just strum. Do everything skilfully, and one of the ways to learn about it is to do things in the garden, play games and so on. Now I suggest this and you say, 'I don't want to garden, it bores me.' What are you going to do with such a person?

Questioner: Find out why he or she won't do it.

KRISHNAMURTI: And then what?

Questioner: There might be a reason why . . .

KRISHNAMURTI: Find out. He says to you, 'I don't like it, I'm bored with it.'

Questioner: You have a right not to, if you don't want to.

KRISHNAMURTI: You are all too quick with answers. I don't want to garden and I don't want to work in the kitchen. You see what happens – gradually I withdraw. And round me I am going to collect people who don't want to do things.

Questioner: That's just one thing you don't want to do.

KRISHNAMURTI: But why not? Intelligence says you must be good at these things and not say, 'I don't want to play games.' You are going to live here much more than you do at home – this is your home, my home, other people's home; it is our home. Our home means also the garden, the lawn, the planting of the trees, the looking after the trees. As I am going to live here, I can't say, 'I don't want to look after the garden.' It is our home, I can't leave it to you. How will you show me or help me to learn that we must do things together, or learn about doing things together. It is as much your responsibility as Mrs Simmons', or someone else's. How will you help me, who says, 'I am bored with games – leave me alone with my pop music or with my book. As I feel at home, I am going to leave my pyjamas on the floor in my room.' What will you do? 'I'm going to leave my shoes in the corridor, or I'll leave my room untidy, I don't care.

At home in California, in London, in Paris, I behave as I want to. Here, why are you telling me what I should do?' And then somebody comes along and tells you. 'Please, don't do that.' You reply, 'You are authoritarian, this is our home I can do whatever I like.'

So how will you teach or help me to learn that to live intelligently implies playing games, looking after the garden, studying, doing things with one's hands, not just with one's brain. Personally, I like to do everything, gardening, milking cows, looking after chickens, looking after babies, changing diapers – I have done all kinds of things. I like it, nobody imposes it on me, and that's the way to live, that's the most intelligent way: having the capacity to do things.

Now what will you do with a person in this school, who says, 'I'm going to leave my room as I like – I sleep in it. I am orderly because I can find what I want among this disorder.' Where do you start learning? We all want to live together, be happy together, do things together – life is doing things together. So please tell me how you propose to learn about all this.

Questioner: You start in a spirit of co-operation.

KRISHNAMURTI: If you have got it, how are you going to help me to learn about it?

Questioner: You have to make a rule.

KRISHNAMURTI: Then what happens? The moment you make a rule I'm going to break it, because I want to be free. People went to America because they did not like various impositions, they said they wanted to be free. They left the old country and went to a new country. They said, 'We'll start anew, no bishops, no kings.' Gradually the monster has grown there too.

So do we see the importance of having a good brain that can think, that can study, that can observe and learn objectively, sanely?

Questioner: Sir, what happens if we are born with an insufficient brain?

KRISHNAMURTI: If you are born with an insufficient brain, then I'm afraid there is nothing much you can do.

Questioner: You talk about it as if there is something we can do.

KRISHNAMURTI: Obviously, because if we have got insufficient brains we are not necessarily moronic.

Questioner: I mean feeble-minded.

KRISHNAMURTI: If you are feeble-minded, this can be corrected by recognizing it. I'm going to do something about it, I don't just say, 'I am feeble-minded' and sit back.

Questioner: Then what do you do?

KRISHNAMURTI: Learn that I am feeble-minded.

Questioner: Some people have a greater capacity to do things than others.

KRISHNAMURTI: So learn. If I have the capacity to do one thing better than another, it can lead to lop-sided living. I am a human being, I've got extraordinary capacities. I must exercise all those capacities, otherwise I'm not a human being. I become merely a technician. If you say, 'I'm not really interested in anything like music, or looking at the loveliness of the day – leave me with my mathematics,' then I say, 'You are feeble-minded.'

Questioner: But isn't there something such as inherent capacity that we are born with?

KRISHNAMURTI: Anything can be changed.

Questioner: Can we all be Beethovens?

KRISHNAMURTI: I want to learn: I don't want to be like anybody, I don't want to become like Christ or Buddha or Beethoven or Einstein! I want to see things differently, have a way of living entirely differently. As a group of people living together, who are encouraged to feel that here is their home, what will you do if somebody says, 'Sorry, I don't feel like working in the garden, ever?'

Questioner: (1) Maybe it's not their home.

Questioner: (2) I suppose it's no good splitting up into groups? — those who like gardening and those who like doing something else.

Questioner: (3) If someone doesn't like gardening, maybe he doesn't feel this is his home, maybe he doesn't belong here.

KRISHNAMURTI: Right, he doesn't belong here. How will you convey it to him? Will you say: 'You come here to be educated in the real sense of that word and apparently you don't like to be educated; you want to remain a savage.' Will you push him out? He came here too for education and he doesn't know what it means to be educated, he thought only in terms of revolt against the Establishment, against the professor, saying, 'I know everything, who are you to tell me?' And he doesn't know what that word 'co-operation' means. You may have to get rid of him. Will you do that?

Questioner: Does that mean we have to get to like what learning is?

KRISHNAMURTI: That's what we are doing now.

Questioner: That's what we're doing; so we don't have to worry about somebody else.

KRISHNAMURTI: But suppose at the end of four months I still keep my room like a pig-sty, what are you going to do with me?

Questioner: If I really agreed with you that having a clean room is necessary, it wouldn't ever be dirty again.

KRISHNAMURTI: But you don't. You are all children, with heavy bodies, with a lot of kick, but children.

Questioner: Well then, what's the reason?

KRISHNAMURTI: Have patience to find out, tell me.

Questioner: What would you do? Talk to them?

KRISHNAMURTI: First we come to a place like this to learn. Learning is not only from a book, but learning together what co-operation means. And learning together what it means to find out that man has always sought security: security in God, in marriage, socially – in everything man wants security. Security means passing an exam, getting a degree: that gives you the promise of security. Here is a place to find out if there is such a thing as security. Here is a place where we are going to educate ourselves, which means learning together what it means to co-operate, what it means to find out what love is. We are completely ignorant of so many things.

Questioner: May I ask something? When someone is violent in his practice of yoga – in the way he does it – and you are constantly warning him, mostly this does not help the person to realize his own violence; he may at the time realize it, but he keeps on. In the same way, one could oneself have been doing certain things for a very long time until suddenly one realizes it.

KRISHNAMURTI: True.

Questioner: Is it possible to educate someone who has not gone through a natural kind of maturation, like a plant? So what is the reaction of a person, who has grown a little more, to the person who has not grown? And if the person, for instance, has not grown to the awareness of the need for a still mind, the necessity of a still mind, how can you help another? – you cannot. So how can we act here?

KRISHNAMURTI: He's talking about Yoga. He asks, when you stand this way, take this posture, do you get the idea first, or do you do it as the yoga teacher is saying it? You see the difference? He says, 'Sit this way,' and he shows you. Do you have the image of how he sits and then carry it out, or in the very observing of how he is sitting, are you doing it? As he is showing it to you, do you have the idea of what he's doing and then carry out the idea? Or are you doing it as he is showing it to you? Which do you do?

Questioner: We do it while he's showing it.

KRISHNAMURTI: Which means what? Go into it. Which means, doesn't it? that you are listening very carefully to what he's saying – the very listening is the doing. Not first listen, then have the idea, and then carry out the idea – which is entirely different. That needs education, that needs growth.

Look, I have done yoga for many years. I've had several yoga teachers, and I did it as they told me; which means there was no contradiction between the doing and the listening. If you first create the idea, the image, then it will take an infinitely long time, then you need practice. But if the teacher says, 'Do this' and you do it, you are *doing* it. You may do it badly, but you are doing it. See the importance of this. Most of us listen, then create an idea, and then carry out the idea. Here, if you listen and do, the idea is gone. The cultivation of the idea and carrying out the idea needs time – which is called maturity, growth.

Questioner: Let us say someone is doing a yoga posture and I say, 'Be violent, try to force it,' that would be preventing them to see . . .

KRISHNAMURTI: I'll show you something – touch the floor with your hands. Say, you've never done it, you may not be able to do that. What do you do? You listen, you may not be able to touch the floor, but you are doing it. The actual doing of it may take a little time, but the 'doing of it' is there already.

Questioner: You haven't completed it, but you're on the way to doing it.

KRISHNAMURTI: That's it.

Questioner: Because you're not resisting.

KRISHNAMURTI: The moment you have an idea you are already resisting.

Questioner: It would be the same about co-operation.

KRISHNAMURTI: About everything.

Questioner: (1) But in Yoga suppose he attempts to do something that's wrong . . .

Questioner: (2) Maybe you have to do it anyway, because if you don't do what he does, you can't find out if it's wrong.

KRISHNAMURTI: Therefore you have to find out if he is the right teacher. I'm not a professional but I've done a great deal of yoga. There is a teacher who is supposed to be the teacher of other teachers. He says, 'To do yoga properly, is to do it without any effort. If there is an effort it's not yoga.' See the reason for it. Your body is not subtle, it's rigid, therefore it takes a week or more, but don't force it. If you force, then you exert muscles in a wrong direction, which is bad for them; so do it very gently, take a week, a month, but do it slowly. If the teacher tells you, 'Sit that way,' you may do it wrongly, but begin, don't carry out the *idea*. In the same way, you listen to the feeling of co-operation, and you already have it if you're listening to it. Don't create an idea about co-operation and then carry that idea out.

Questioner: Can we take orderliness, for instance?

KRISHNAMURTI: Yes. We need order; if you are untidy, if you are unpunctual, we can't live together, it'll become impossible. We have to have a certain order. Don't create a picture of it: that I want order and you don't want order. We have to live together in a place like this. To live together implies order. So I have to have order. Do you listen to it without any resistance, or are you going to fight it? Please listen to what is being said without any resistance, knowing that living together needs order. If I don't bathe and I say,

44

'What's wrong with it? I'm all right. I like my smell' – then we create disorder.

Are you listening now to the word 'co-operation', to the word 'order', not creating a picture of it? – then you are immediately orderly.

Questioner: Don't words like order and co-operation mean something to us, in so far as we've experienced them?

KRISHNAMURTI: Yes, of course they do. Which means what? You've already made a picture, had an experience of what order is, what co-operation is, and that becomes the resistance. Whereas if we say, 'Look, let's find out, learn what it means to be orderly, what it means to co-operate,' then we can't have a conclusion about it, because we're learning. If the yoga teacher says to you, 'Sit this way,' you may not be able to, it may take a week or a month, but the way you listen to it is far more important than sitting rightly. The sitting rightly will come, but the listening to what he says is instantaneous.

Questioner: Usually for us to listen that way, we have to have a great deal of confidence.

KRISHNAMURTI: Why should you have confidence? I'm telling you and you listen. Why should you have confidence in me?

Questioner: Because you might be telling me to kill.

KRISHNAMURTI: Why should you have confidence in me? First learn the art of listening, learn – not from me. Because I don't *know,* I may say things that are wrong; therefore listen to find out what is true and what is false, which is to become sensitive. You cannot become sensitive – which is intelligence – if you are obstinate, if you resist when someone says to you: 'This is what I think.' The important thing is the art of listening.

Questioner: But if someone is telling you what they *think, isn't that* them *telling* you?

KRISHNAMURTI: Of course. I'm your yoga teacher, I'm supposed to know something about it, I may not know the whole of it, but I know a little bit of it and I teach you what I know. And in teaching you I'm also learning.

3

What does it mean to live together intelligently? Freedom and being open to learn. Co-operation. Orderliness.

KRISHNAMURTI: The other day we were discussing what Brockwood Park is trying to do. We were saying that it has come into being in order to bring about intelligence, if that is possible. The word 'intelligence' means having the faculty of understanding – to understand not only each other, but also what co-operation means, what freedom, what discipline and order mean. We said intelligence implies freedom. That freedom is not yours or mine – but freedom. Let's be very clear on this point. Please stop me if you don't understand. Don't be silent and then say afterwards, 'I disagree with you.' We are trying to find out together.

As we happen to be a small community, what does it mean to live together intelligently? Obviously the first thing is that there should be freedom between you and me and the others. Freedom doesn't mean doing what you want to do, because if each one of us did what he wanted there would be chaos here. Or a few of you would form a group thinking this is what we want to do in freedom, as opposed to another group. That is not freedom either.

You may say, 'I think it is freedom to do what I like, because at home I do what I like, there is nobody to say "don't do it", and if they did I would revolt, get angry, run away.' To do what one likes is really quite impossible. Because what one likes may be temporary, a passing desire, and if we all did what we liked without considering the others, we couldn't live together. So intelligence implies freedom to find out how to live together. You don't impose on me and I don't impose on you. Do see the responsibilities. And free-

47

dom implies that together we understand what the implications of authority are. If I sit up late and you tell me it's time to go to bed, don't call that authoritarian: that would be unintelligent. Because both of us have gone into the question of going to bed at a fixed hour, we have agreed. Our relationship then is not authoritarian, not nagging, but through intelligence. We have discussed what time to go to bed and intelligence is telling us, not authority. If I react to your telling me in a friendly way or with annoyance – whether you tell me rudely or politely – it is my lack of intelligence. I don't know if you see that.

Questioner: There is also a lack of intelligence in a person who tells me abruptly.

KRISHNAMURTI: Of course, none of us is completely intelligent. We are learning – learning the nature, the quality of intelligence. I get angry and say things, and I am aware that I am silly, which is part of intelligence. Next time I will be careful, I will be watchful. So you see, co-operation is an understanding of intelligence.

Questioner: I wonder who is seeing, who is watching?

KRISHNAMURTI: Yourself. I am angry with you, I say, 'Please go to bed at eleven, I have told you ten times.' I get irritated and I say to myself, 'How silly of me to get irritated with a person who hasn't got the intelligence to see and after discussing it is still late.' I see I've got angry. What's the difficulty?

Questioner: I am wondering if it's possible to look without the conditioning – the watcher is still in the conditioning.

KRISHNAMURTI: No, don't go into the complex problem of the observer. We'll come to that a little later, I'm not disregarding what you're saying, but we are talking now of the quality of intelligence that co-operates.

Questioner: If someone says you are authoritarian, of course that's a reaction; but it is also a reaction to get angry. So why not say, 'Don't be angry.'

KRISHNAMURTI: Of course. We are living together, we are trying to see, to help each other, learn from each other. If you refuse to learn because you think you are better, what are we going to do? The younger people think they know everything; what are you going to do if they say, 'I disagree with you' and stick to it.

Questioner: We're going to go into it.

KRISHNAMURTI: But if they refuse to go into it.

Questioner: That's what we are doing now, laying the foundations for that.

KRISHNAMURTI: That's just it, we are trying to lay the foundations so that we can live together intelligently. Not, you live intelligently and you tell me; or I tell you, but *together*. It's our responsibility together to be intelligent. Now what does that word mean? According to the dictionary it means to understand, to have the faculty of understanding.

Questioner: To choose between different courses is what it literally means.

KRISHNAMURTI: Yes, you must have the faculty to choose and that faculty must be intelligent. If I choose out of prejudice it's not intelligence. So if we are laying the foundations of an environment in which our principal concern is to live together intelligently, this demands not only freedom, but self-critical awareness. I must be aware of what I am doing, why I'm doing it, of the consequence of that action; not be obstinate and say, 'This is right! This is what I think! I'll stick to it.' Then you stop learning, then we have no relationship.

Do you see this? Don't agree with me unless you really see it. My problem is: we want to live here happily, freely and intelligently, which we can't do in the world, because the world is brutal, thoughtless. Here we want to create an atmosphere, an environment, build a foundation where we live together, happily, intelligently, in co-operation. I am explaining what intelligent living together means. Find out, don't be silent and then go your own way afterwards. Discuss with me, so that we both learn what it is to be intelligent and live together in co-operation. Intelligence implies the faculty of understanding freedom, and all of us want to be free. We don't want to be under the control of any tyranny, whether of the family or of someone else. And we are trying to find out how to live together freely. I can stay by myself in my loneliness, in my room, dissociated from everybody; that may be what I call my freedom, but I can't live that way. We are human beings in relationship with each other, therefore we must understand what it means to live together in freedom. And that demands intelligence.

Now, how are we going to do this? You might have an idea of freedom and I have another idea of it. So I say to myself, 'I don't know what it means, I'm going to find out.' You see the difference? If you start by saying, 'I know what freedom means', it is finished – I don't know if you see this? – then you are not intelligent enough to learn about it.

Questioner: You are living in your own tyranny then.

KRISHNAMURTI: Of course, you are living in your own soup, which is not very interesting. So we must both understand what it means to be free. Do you want to learn about it? Or do you say, 'Don't teach me, I know all about it.' When you say that you are already unintelligent, because you are not learning, you are fixed in your idea of what you think is freedom. I want to learn what it means to live together in freedom; therefore the first thing is not to say to myself, 'I know what it means.' So do you want to learn what freedom means? Because that's what we want to do at Brockwood.

I'll show you why. In freedom you can discover new

things. In the world of science there must be freedom to discover new things. In human relationship, here, we are discovering, or learning, new things about ourselves. If I am fixed in my opinion, I can't learn. So I must be very careful, be aware of my fixed opinions or judgements; because this is what the world is doing and it's not learning. They have fixed ideas, opinions, conclusions from which they won't budge. And there are young people revolting against that; yet they have their own opinions, their prejudices, their fixed conclusions, so they are like the old.

Questioner: What do you do then if people have their fixed opinions?

KRISHNAMURTI: People who have opinions, judgements, conclusions which they hold on to are incapable of living together freely, with intelligence. So have you opinions, judgements, conclusions, a tradition? All these things I have but I am going to learn. You see the difference? After all, this is a place in which we are being educated, not only about geography and history, mathematics and so on, but we are educating ourselves with the help of each other to be highly intelligent when we leave. You may never leave, you may want to become a teacher here, that's up to you.

This is an educational centre; an educational centre implies the cultivation of intelligence – which is the subtlety of understanding, the faculty to choose. To choose the right course the mind must be free from every form of prejudice, every form of conclusion. Do you want a place like this where you can be educated, freely, happily, in intelligence? Which means, really, co-operation, doesn't it? I cannot co-operate with you if I emphasize my peculiarities. You understand? If I give importance to length of hair and make that the symbol of revolt, follow the consequences of it. Long hair is now the fashion. Length of hair is a symbol of revolt, a symbol of doing what one likes, because the old generation are short haired: it is a symbol of self-assertive aggression, a symbol of beauty. All these are implied in it, aren't they? A symbol of revolt against war, of revolt against the established order. Do you wear your hair long because it's beautiful?

Questioner: It's like a trap. There are two things: short hair is the Establishment, long hair is anti-Establishment.

KRISHNAMURTI: I don't say, 'Long hair is right' or 'Short hair is right'. I am asking you: do you wear it because it looks beautiful?

Questioner: Well, let's say it makes me feel more comfortable.

KRISHNAMURTI: Now go into it very carefully. It makes you feel comfortable. Suppose you sit next to me, unwashed, dirty, smelly and I say I don't want to sit next to you. If it is comfortable to you it must also be comfortable to me, who am sitting at the table next to you.

Questioner: Right.

KRISHNAMURTI: Long hair does look very nice if it is kept properly – not hanging all over the face – do you do it for that reason?

Questioner: I don't know if I do it specifically for that reason, to have nice shiny hair.

KRISHNAMURTI: Then why do you keep it long?

Questioner: It feels good in the wind and it feels good in the water.

KRISHNAMURTI: All right, but you are not in the wind all the time. You have to sit next to me. You are not living alone in this world. We are learning to live together with intelligence, in freedom.

Questioner: Yes, but I can see if bugs are crawling out of the hair, if the hair is just left to grow, I can see why you react on your part if you are sitting next to it.

KRISHNAMURTI: Wait, I've told you to watch it. As long as it is clean and really looks nice, doesn't smell, what's wrong with it? In Ceylon the men have long hair, they put circular combs in it to keep it tidy and it looks very nice. Are you going to go about like that, with a comb in it? *(Laughter.)* What's wrong? You see, you are prejudiced, that's what I am getting at.

Questioner: It's not really prejudice. I don't have anything against you if you go around with a comb in your hair.

KRISHNAMURTI: As I have to live with you, if you are smelly, if you are untidy, I object to it.

Questioner: Right. But there's a little confusion for me about the word 'tidy'.

KRISHNAMURTI: So if you feel long hair is right, then wear it. But it means that you have to be clean. Or, do you wear it as a symbol of your revolt against the Establishment? And because I have short hair, does it mean I am accepting the Establishment? See the danger. So why are you wearing long hair? You haven't answered me. Do you do it because everybody does it? – which is imitation, conformity, which is unintelligent. Know what you are doing. Is it part of intelligence? If you said, 'Look, I'm growing my hair because I like it, it looks nice, it's clean', I'd accept it immediately. But if you're wearing it as a symbol, then I want to know what that symbol is, because I've got to live with you. Your symbol may mean death to me! I want to find out.

Questioner: But isn't there also kinship with your generation?

KRISHNAMURTI: But know why you are doing it. Kinship with your generation – is that right?

Questioner: Friendship, being related to . . .

KRISHNAMURTI: If you feel related to the long-haired ones and not to the short-haired ones, do you see what you are doing? It means you are creating division, which the older generation has created, and therefore you are following in their footsteps. So you are creating as much destruction as

53

they did. Then to wear the symbol of peace on your shirt means nothing. So what I'm saying is, if we are going to live together in intelligence and freedom, we must both know what we are doing and why we are doing it. Not just cover it up with a lot of words, because that is not intelligence. Why do we have vegetarian food in this place? Do you ask that? You raised the word 'tidy'. Do you know what it means to be orderly? You don't, do you?

Questioner : If I did I wouldn't be here.

KRISHNAMURTI: We are going to go into it. To think in an orderly way, to think clearly, to act clearly. Not: to think one thing and do something else; but to think very clearly, objectively, sanely, that is orderly, isn't it? I'm going to bring that word 'tidy' into this. To dress neatly is orderly, isn't it?

Questioner : I'm not sure.

KRISHNAMURTI: What is it you are not sure of? You come into the dining-room with naked, dirty feet and I'm sitting next to you. I don't like it because it's not clean, I like to be clean. And you say, that's a prejudice. Is it? Every animal wants to be clean.

Questioner : Every animal has naked feet too.

KRISHNAMURTI: But it is clean. It's always keeping clean – you've seen it licking itself. Come with clean feet! – which means keep the floor clean.

4

Education to face the world. The problem of sex. Affection.

KRISHNAMURTI: What kind of human being are you going to be when you go out into the world? You will have to face so many problems, won't you? Not only economic, social, environmental problems, but also problems of relationship, sex, of how to live intelligently, with great love and affection and not be smothered, corrupted by society. Here, in this school, we are more or less protected and among friends; there can be trust, we are familiar with each other's idiosyncrasies, prejudices, inclinations and tendencies, but when we go out into the world we do not know anybody and we are facing a monstrous world.

We have to find out how we are going to meet all this, what kind of mind or intelligence is going to face this. So education becomes of the greatest importance. Education being not merely the acquisition of technical knowledge, but the understanding, with sensitivity and intelligence, of the whole problem of living – in which is included death, love, sex, meditation, relationship, and also conflict, anger, brutality and all the rest of it – that is the whole structure of human existence.

If we could face just one issue completely, go into it very deeply, then perhaps we shall be able to relate it to all the others. No problem is something separate, all by itself. It is related to other issues, other problems, other affairs. So if we can take one human problem and enquire into it freely, then we shall be able to see the connection with all other problems. So what shall we talk about together?

Questioner: What is the purpose of life?

KRISHNAMURTI: It was made very clear the other day that to have a purpose implies a direction: you fix a direction and avoid everything else. If I say, 'I want to go to "The Grove" this morning because there are marvellous flowers there', then my whole attention is on getting there and therefore I resist everything else. Similarly, to ask what is the purpose of life is to invite more contradiction, more conflict. I don't know if you really see that?

Questioner: Perhaps the real difficulty is communication?

KRISHNAMURTI: Is that our difficulty? When you want to say something, you say it, don't you?

Questioner: Yes, but communication is to do something together.

KRISHNAMURTI: You say communication means doing something together – understanding together, creating together. Is that what you want to discuss?

Questioner: (1) Perhaps we have a desire to do things together because we don't feel we can stand alone?

Questioner: (2) So perhaps we can discuss right relationship?

Questioner: (3) It seems that we are so scattered in our thinking.

KRISHNAMURTI: Surely your thoughts are not scattered when you are interested. Do tell me, what interests you?

Questioner: Happiness.

KRISHNAMURTI: Is that what you are all interested in? – happiness, enjoyment, pleasure, having a good time? Is that what you are going to be interested in not only now when you are adolescent, but right through life? What are you all going to do? Just seek happiness, saying, 'If I could have more jewels, more sex, more of this or that I would be happy' – is that what you all want?

Questioner: I could be interested in certain other aspects of life, such as politics.

56

KRISHNAMURTI: All right, but if you are interested in politics are you only concerned with one segment of life? If you are really interested in politics you have to be interested in the whole movement of existence and not regard politics as something entirely separate, as most politicians do.

Questioner: I could be interested in being an engineer, but also in living as a human being.

KRISHNAMURTI: So you are interested in engineering but also in understanding the whole of life. Now which do you consider the most important, the most vital – without putting them in opposition?

Questioner: The whole, everything.

KRISHNAMURTI: Which includes religion – you follow? If you emphasize engineering and disregard all the rest, then you are a lop-sided human being; in fact you are not a human being at all, just a technician. So knowing that, what shall we take to discuss, so that enquiring into it we shall understand that all other problems are included also? Which subject shall we take? Is sex a tremendous problem to you, an issue?

Questioner: Well, it doesn't have to be an issue for me, but other people around me make it an issue.

KRISHNAMURTI: Do they? Can they?

Questioner: Surely they can!

KRISHNAMURTI: All right. You are walking down the street and the girls are attracted to you and you say the blame lies with the girls and you are quite blameless!

Questioner: No, it's not quite that. But take sexual relationship. If I'm having a sexual relationship with someone and other people know about it, then somehow they can make it into a problem.

KRISHNAMURTI: Wait a minute. You are here in a school,

a so-called Educational Centre; you are sent here by your parents and you have also said you want to come here. So you are not just a separate individual, doing what you like, you are responsible for this place. It is your home and you are responsible for it, for the house and the garden and for keeping it orderly. And you are responsible to your parents, to the people here, to the neighbours – the whole of it. And naturally people are watching what is going on here. They have given money, they have children here, there are the neighbours, the visitors, the people who work here who are interested, they are all watching.

So if I want to have a sexual affair with someone here, I have to be fully awake to all the dangers of it and also to all the possible consequences of it. If I'm having an affair with someone here, then the staff who are responsible to your parents, to the neighbourhood and for the welfare of the school, are bound to be concerned, aren't they? They are bound to watch you very carefully; that's not being authoritarian, is it?

Questioner: Does anyone else have to know about it? And is it necessarily harmful?

KRISHNAMURTI: Can you possibly keep it a secret in a place like this? We have not said it is harmful, or not. We are looking at it and someone says that the other person is to blame. The people who are in charge are keeping an eye on you and they say, 'Now look, see what is happening, what you are doing.' Is that being authoritarian? Who is making the problem? Are you making the problem, or the people who are concerned for the whole place? You have to be sensitive; you have to know you can't do certain things. If there's a baby, what will happen?

Questioner: The one who has the baby is responsible.

KRISHNAMURTI: So the mother has the problem?

Questioner: And the father too.

58

KRISHNAMURTI: And what happens about all the other people concerned, the parents, the school, the neighbourhood? Perhaps the parents are away in India, or America; did they send you here to produce children who have to be looked after?

Questioner: But then, Sir, if boys and girls want to have sexual relationship, it creates a conflict if you can't do it.

KRISHNAMURTI: So, you do it. And then what?

Questioner: Well, then it becomes a problem.

KRISHNAMURTI: What makes the problem?

Questioner: It's a problem in that the students are saying contradictory things. On the one hand they don't want to conform, and on the other hand they say, 'Why can't I do what I want to do?', which is conforming.

KRISHNAMURTI: Both sides are saying that. We have to go a little deeper. Please put yourself in the place of the parent who has sent a son or daughter here to be educated, or in the place of the person who is responsible for running this place, with the boys and girls together. What is your responsibility? *(Pause.)* You see how you become silent, how you smile differently?

Questioner: Even if a mother and a father are very concerned about their child, it doesn't necessarily mean that they stop them having a sexual relationship.

KRISHNAMURTI: That is something different. The point is that we are here, in this school, boys and girls together. And perhaps all your glands are working at top speed because of biological urges, and there is all the excitement of showing off, showing one's body and all the rest of it. You know it all much better than I do. Now, what is going to happen, in a place like this? Here you are told to enquire into conformity, to understand it, to use your minds, your intelligence. Then this sexual problem arises, the sex instinct is aroused

59

in a place where lots of boys and girls are together. What are you going to do? Pursue your biological urge secretly or openly? Come on, do discuss this.

Questioner: Well, in America many of the students would say, 'Yes.'

KRISHNAMURTI: I know that many of the students in America, or France, or in the universities here say, 'That's none of your business.'

Questioner: And if you put it the other way round, if you say, 'I won't pursue my biological urge,' what then?

KRISHNAMURTI: First let us see what is involved in the whole of it – not just my personal biological urge. Don't just say that the parents and the people who are concerned about this place are making me conform, that they are authoritarian. This place is in the public eye. The public eye may be corrupt, stupid, but if this centre gets a bad name then the whole future of the school is in jeopardy; then the place may have to shut down. You must take all this into consideration. So what will you do with your biological urge? Come on, let's discuss it. What will you do? You have investigated so far, you have thought about your parents, your responsibility here, the responsibilities to the parents of those who are in charge, of the neighbourhood, of the future of the school.

Questioner: But aren't the students equally in charge here, not only the staff?

KRISHNAMURTI: I have said that. This is your home, the home of all of you, and therefore you are all responsible for what happens here. So, what is your action then? Knowing that biologically everything is supercharged, what will you do? After all, you read the magazines, the newspapers, the stories, you go to the cinema, you've seen the half-naked girls and you know about the whole thing. Now what is your responsibility? Please discuss with me. That is one of the problems of life and you don't want to face it. But you can't brush it under the carpet. How are you going to deal with a problem of that kind with a mind that is not completely mature? Because you are all very young, you understand? Your minds have not yet become tremendously active, sensitive and intelligent. You are faced with this problem and naturally you want to avoid it. There is fear and apprehension.

How is your mind going to be intelligent enough to deal with it? Because society all around you is pushing you in that one direction, through clothes, fashion – everything leads towards sex. In India kissing on the screen is not allowed. When you go out into the world the problem is there and even if you are married it is there. So how will you have an intelligence that will deal with this problem without any kind of resistance, conflict or suppression? If you yield to it, it will become another form of neurosis; if you suppress it, it will also lead to neurosis; if you resist it, it will do terrible things to you. You know what happens to people who resist all these things? They become bottled up, they get angry about nothing, they become hysterical.

So how can one bring about a mind that is capable of neither resisting, suppressing, nor yielding? This is a real problem. How do you have a mind that is sensitive, alert, sharp and also extraordinarily capable of responding to beauty – the beauty of a woman or of a child? How do you come by it?

When you have examined a problem thoroughly and you come to this point, what do you do? You say, don't you: 'I don't know what to do,' and then you say, 'Let's drop it.' You follow? To live a life without effort, without conformity, without suppression, without resistance, without following the crowd – going to parties, the whole stupefying process of modern existence: that is real education.

Now watch! – because this issue will exist right through life. As we have said, if you suppress it there is danger it will explode in other directions; and if you yield, or play tricks with it, it will destroy you, destroy the mind.

So the mind has learnt not to suppress and not to yield, not to make an immense problem of it. Is this clear to you? Does it mean anything to you? Or do you say: 'Let him talk, we'll have our pleasures, we'll get married, carry on, and then we'll face it'?

Have you ever asked why human beings give such extraordinary importance to this one thing, to sex? Throughout the world it is much more important than money, much more important than religion. In the West it is talked about freely, exposed. In the East it is all kept behind locked doors, whether one is married or not. Why, do you think, has it become a thing of such colossal importance?

Questioner: (1) Maybe it's because of the pleasure; it is something you can have without money.

Questioner: (2) Could it be that people have a lot of energy in them which they haven't used on other things, and therefore they use it in this direction?

KRISHNAMURTI: Go on, push at it, create together, contribute! Don't just sit there and let me do all the work!

Questioner: It may be an escape from a sorrow, or a problem.

KRISHNAMURTI: So look at it! We have been working together, understanding together, communicating. You have said sex has become so important because of the pleasure, the surplus energy, as an escape from the daily routine. Now is that what is happening to you? I don't say you are having sexual affairs, I'm just asking: is this what your mind is groping after? – seeking pleasure, escaping from the monotony of school, of learning this or that, and therefore your mind goes off, creating images?

Questioner: Is it not also that we are looking for affection? This one thing is not found because people are always pointing out that it is not right.

KRISHNAMURTI: Is this what you are doing? Are you saying that you want affection, you want kindliness, tender-

62

ness, concern, something real, and because you don't get it
you think you'll get it through pleasure, through sex? Of
course you need affection as you need sunshine, rain and
clouds. But why do you *seek* it? Why do you say so-and-so
doesn't show me affection?

Questioner: Because affection makes you feel better.

KRISHNAMURTI: Go deeper.

Questioner: It feeds your ego.

KRISHNAMURTI: Go on, push at it!

*Questioner: You become closer to a person and you want to really get
near to people and know them.*

KRISHNAMURTI: That is, you say you want affection from
others because it makes you feel comfortable and happy, you
feel you can blossom.

Questioner: And also there is something you want to give.

KRISHNAMURTI: Yes, you want to give and to share, all
that. So go on, what does it all mean? I am seeking affection
from others: what does that mean?

Questioner: There is a lack of affection in myself.

KRISHNAMURTI: What does that mean, the lack of affection in yourself? Look, a spring of water is bubbling over all
the time, isn't it? – giving, pouring out. And it is only when
my own spring of affection is not functioning deeply that I
want somebody else to give it to me. Right?

Questioner: It's not always that way.

KRISHNAMURTI: Why do you say, 'Not always'? Please
listen to this carefully. If you have deep affection in yourself
for everything – not just for one, but for everything – love
for the trees, the birds, the flowers, the fields and for human
beings – if you really feel that way, will you even occasion-

ally say, 'I wish someone would show me affection'? Isn't it only when there is emptiness inside you that you want others to be with you?

So you have learnt something, haven't you? Your mind now is actively observing, looking intelligently, and you see that where there is no affection in oneself, you want affection from others. That is translated as sex, relationship, and when that emptiness within seeks a relationship through sex and through a constant companionship, then you become jealous, fearful, angry. You follow? Please see all the consequences of it. So sex isn't the problem. The problem is to have an intelligent mind and in the very observing of all this it becomes highly intelligent and this intelligence will deal with sex. I don't know if you follow? Have you understood it?

Questioner: It also means, in turn, that one can have a sexual relationship without having a problem.

KRISHNAMURTI: I don't say that.

Questioner: I mean, there's a possibility.

KRISHNAMURTI: No, no. I wouldn't put it that way. First, be intelligent, then that intelligence will answer the problem rightly, whatever it is. Have an intelligent mind, not a distorted mind. A distorted mind says, 'That is what I want and I'm going after it.' Which means that it has no concern for the whole, but only for its own little demands – it has not been watching the whole process. So here it is your responsibility to have this intelligence, and if you don't have it, then don't blame somebody else. You know, to live intelligently in this way becomes an extraordinary, a tremendous thing; there is real enjoyment in this. But along the other way you live with fear.

5

Order, discipline and learning. Space and freedom. Need for security,
confidence: the feeling of 'home'. Learning to live together without
authority. Responsibility for each other and the 'home'.
About meditation.

KRISHNAMURTI: In a school like this, what is order and
what is discipline? The word 'discipline' means 'to learn'.
A 'disciple' is one who learns, not who conforms, not who
obeys; he is one who is constantly learning. And when learning ceases and becomes merely accumulation of knowledge
then disorder begins. When we stop learning in our relationship, whether we are studying, playing, or whatever we are
doing, and merely act from the knowledge that we have
accumulated, then disorder comes.

Discipline *is* learning. You say something, such as, 'Don't
give the dogs too much food' or, 'Go to bed early' or, 'Be
punctual', 'Keep the room tidy'. You tell me that and I
am learning. Life, living, is a movement in learning and if I
resist your telling me what to do, the resistance is the assertion of my own particular accumulated knowledge; therefore I cease to learn and so create a conflict between you and
me.

Questioner: Does this apply to students only or to anybody?

KRISHNAMURTI: To life, not only to students, to human
beings.

Questioner: But everybody is not a disciple.

KRISHNAMURTI: Everybody is learning. 'Disciple' means
'one who learns'. But the generally accepted meaning is
that a disciple is one who follows someone, some guru, some

silly person. But both the follower and the one who is followed are not learning.

Questioner: But if we follow somebody who is not silly?

KRISHNAMURTI: You cannot follow *anybody*. The moment you follow somebody you are making yourself an idiot and the one whom you follow is also an idiot – because they have stopped learning. So, what do you do about discipline, about order? Are you learning about *everything*? – not only about geography, history and all the rest of it, but learning about relationship? We are living together in this house, each pulling in a different direction, each wanting something, each resisting somebody else saying, 'Oh, he or she has become authoritarian.' All such assertions, all such resistances, and doing what one thinks one wants to do – does not all that create disorder?

If you say, 'I'm doing what I want to do; I'm being natural; it's my nature and you are not going to tell me what to do' – if you say that, and I say the same, what then takes place? What is our relationship? Can we ever do anything 'naturally'? This is a very serious question, if you follow what I mean. Are you natural, any of you? Of course you are not! You are influenced – by your father, by your mother, by society, by your culture, by the climate, the food, the clothes, the propaganda. You are completely influenced and then you say, 'I must be natural!' It has no meaning. You say, 'I want to do what I think is the right thing' or, 'I am a free person'. You are not! You are not free. Freedom is something tremendous and to start out saying, 'I am free' has no meaning. You don't even know what it means.

Questioner: Then how can you say, 'It is tremendous'?

KRISHNAMURTI: It *is* tremendous when one *is* free, but one is not. Can one realize that one is not free? Freedom means freedom from fear. It means freedom from any form of resistance. Freedom means a movement without isolation. It means having no resistance at all. So are you free? We are frightened, we resist, we are isolated within our own little ideas, wants and desires, obviously. So when you say 'freedom' and 'natural', those two words have no meaning. You can only be free when you have understood how deeply you are conditioned and are free of that conditioning. Then one can be free, then one is natural.

You know what order means? To have a lot of space, doesn't it? In a little room where there is no space it is more difficult to have order. You don't agree? You'll see it in a minute. Somebody told me about an experiment with rats: they put a lot of rats in a very small space and because they had no space they began to kill each other – the mother killed her babies. But we also need space inwardly. More and more cities are becoming overcrowded. You ought to go to India and see some of the big towns like Calcutta, Bombay or Delhi – you have no idea what it is like, the noise, the shouting, the people. They are like ants on the streets and, having no space, they are exploding in violence.

Here we must have space; the house itself is limited in size, so what will you do? Outwardly there is limited space and also how are you going to have inward space? You understand what I mean by inward space? Our minds are so crowded with a thousand ideas there is no space at all, even between two thoughts, between two ideas; between two emotions there is no space, no interval. But unless you have space there is no order. Order means learning, doesn't it? Learning about everything. So, if somebody tells me I am a fool, I want to learn the truth of it; I want to find out. I don't merely resist it and say, 'You're another.' I want to see, I want to listen, to learn. Therefore, learning brings order and resistance brings disorder.

So though outwardly I may not have space, because the world is getting more and more crowded, I want to see if I can have space inwardly. If I have no space inwardly, then I am bound to create disorder. What do you say to this? Here we are, a group of teenagers and they revolt against the established order, which is natural, inevitable. We have

67

come here with those ideas, those feelings, and anybody who tells us anything we call 'authoritarian'. So what are we going to do?

How do we live differently here, act differently, be happy differently? Otherwise, you know what is going to happen? You will be thrown into the jungle of the world, thrown to a lot of wolves and you will be destroyed. In India, about three to four thousand people apply for every job. You understand what that means? They advertised for a cook and do you know who applied? – B.A.s, M.A.s and Ph.Ds! And it is going to get worse, right throughout the world.

So at a school of this kind we *have* to learn. I am using the word 'learn' in the right sense: to find out, explore relationship, because after all that is how we live. Society is the relationship between man and man. And it is essential that we learn here how to live, what relationship is, what love is. We must learn, not just say, 'This is love' or, 'That's not love' or, 'This is authority', 'That's not authority' – all those absurd statements have no meaning. But if we can actually learn together, then I think that this school has some meaning.

In India, at the school in the south, there are little boys from the ages of six up to eighteen, and we talk about everything. In India the word 'meditation' is a tremendous word. There meditation has some meaning. And while I was talking about it, there they were, a whole group of boys, and yet they sat completely still. It was extraordinary how they did it! They shut their eyes, sat cross-legged and were absolutely quiet. It is part of the tradition there that you must meditate – whatever that may mean to them. You must sit quite still, and you must have a good feeling about life ... So how are we, all of us, going to create this together? Not you alone or Mrs Simmons, or me – but all of us together. How can we do this?

Questioner: (1) Is it only together that we can do this?

Questioner: (2) Did you say, ' Not individually, but together' ?

KRISHNAMURTI: Together. You know what the word 'individual' means? – indivisible. An individual means one who is not divisible in himself. But we *are* divisible, we are broken up, we are not individuals. We are little fragments, broken, divided. Look, where does one feel completely secure, safe, protected? And you must have complete security.

Questioner: When you have trust in another?

KRISHNAMURTI: Yes, and also at home, don't you? Home is supposed to be that place where you are completely safe, which you can trust, where you are protected. *This* is your home, isn't it? – for eight months of the year this is your home. But you don't feel secure here, do you?

Questioner: I do.

KRISHNAMURTI: Do you? That's good. But do you all? See what it means to be completely at home, where you are completely secure. The brain demands security; otherwise it can't function efficiently, clearly. It is only when the brain cells feel insecure that one becomes neurotic; one goes off balance. And this is a place where you are *at home*, where you are completely safe.

Questioner: What do you do if this isn't so?

KRISHNAMURTI: I'm coming to that. One needs safety, protection, trust, confidence and a feeling that you can do anything without destroying this. In a place like this you don't feel at home in that sense, do you? Who is going to make it for you? You understand what I'm talking about? Who is going to provide you with this environment of complete protection? I don't think you understand it. Do you know what it means, to be completely protected? You know how a baby needs complete protection, otherwise it cries? It must have its food regularly, it must be washed, taken care of, otherwise it is harmed. Now we are growing up and who is going to provide this home for us? Mrs Simmons, or somebody like me? The day after tomorrow I'm gone. So who is going to provide it for us?

Questioner: All of us.

KRISHNAMURTI: You are going to create it yourselves, you are going to build it. And if you don't build it, it is your fault. You can't say to Mrs Simmons, 'I want complete security and you are not providing it for me.' This is your home and you are building it, you are creating it. If you don't feel at home here it is your fault. Find out about it, bring it about. Bring about this feeling that you are completely at home.

Questioner: Could you go into this question of security because I think we don't understand it. Security for what? Not security for an idea. You see, we identify ourselves with an idea.

KRISHNAMURTI: No! Security, feeling completely safe, security not with ideas but with people. Don't you know what it means?

Questioner: (1) I'm not sure.

Questioner: (2) It's something we don't know. Some of us have come here because we have ideas about it.

KRISHNAMURTI: First of all look! I haven't studied neurology and the structure of the brain, but just watch yourself and you can easily find out. Where the brain feels completely at rest, safe, protected, it functions perfectly, beautifully. Have you ever tried it? It thinks very clearly, can learn very quickly, everything functions beautifully, without friction – that is safety. That is to be completely secure. The brain cells themselves feel there is no conflict. Why should you be in conflict with me or I with you?

When you tell me: 'Keep the room in order', why should I feel, 'Oh, how terrible'? Why shouldn't I be told that? But it creates a conflict in me. Why? Because I have stopped

learning. Are we meeting each other? It is your home and
you have to build it, not somebody else. It is where you feel
completely safe, otherwise you can't learn properly, otherwise you reduce this place to something just like the outside
world, where each one is against the other. Safety means the
brain-cells themselves are in perfect harmony, in perfect
equilibrium, in a sense of being healthy, quiet. *That* is home;
and this place *is* your home. If you don't make it so, it is
your fault. And if you see disorder in your own room, you
have to make order there because it is your home.

So you can never say, 'I'm going to leave this place,'
because it's your home (though you may have to leave it one
day). Do you know what that does when you feel completely
at home, without fear, where you are open, where you are
trusting? Not that you must have trust *in* somebody, but
have the capacity of trusting, of generosity – it doesn't
matter what the other does. I don't know if you are following all this?

*Questioner: When you say, 'It does not matter what the other does',
what do you mean?*

KRISHNAMURTI: Look, you tell me something. Why do
you tell me?

Questioner: Because it's your idea of what is needed.

KRISHNAMURTI: No, no. Why do you or Mrs Simmons
tell me to keep my room in order? Before I say that I will or
I won't, find out why you are telling me that.

Questioner: (1) Because you're not doing it.

Questioner: (2) Because they like order.

KRISHNAMURTI: No. You haven't understood my question. Do listen to it before you answer. I've told you ten
times to keep your room in order and the eleventh time I get
irritated. Then you say I'm bossy. Now, why have I told you
this at all? Find out why. Is it because I want to express my

egotism, my idea of what order is, my idea that you should, behave in this way? Saying, 'Go to bed', 'Be punctual', imposing my idea on your idea. You answer, 'Why should I keep my room in order? Who are you? It is *my* room.' So what takes place then?

Questioner: A struggle.

KRISHNAMURTI: Which means what?

Questioner: Confusion . . .

KRISHNAMURTI: It means, really, that you don't feel at home. You are not learning. Right? Conflict exists only when you are not learning. You come and tell me: 'Keep your room in order', and I listen to you, I learn. And you also find out why you are telling me. Do you follow what I mean? If you want to burn the place down . . . it's your home. If you want to keep the gardens, the house, the rooms untidy and have a messy way of eating, well, it's your home. But if somebody tells me: 'Don't put your feet on the table when you're eating', I say 'Quite right.' I learn.

Questioner: If somebody says to me: ' This is your country . . .'

KRISHNAMURTI: Oh no. Please don't extend it. It is not 'my country'. I am talking about a home. If somebody tells me it is my country and for that country I must kill someone, that's sheer nonsense . . .

Questioner: But can one be learning in that relationship too?

KRISHNAMURTI: Of course! Learning means learning.

Questioner: Yes, but there is also resistance.

KRISHNAMURTI: No, no. You haven't understood the meaning.

Questioner: I don't go and kill.

KRISHNAMURTI: We are discussing a school, living together *here*. If I know how to live here, learn here, then I will know what to do when the Government or the State says: 'Go and kill somebody.' If I don't know how to learn to live, I shan't be able to reply properly.

Questioner: There's something I don't really have straight. If I walk around and I don't wear shoes and somebody says, 'You should wear shoes . . .'

KRISHNAMURTI: What happens? You don't wear shoes and I come along and say, 'Please put on your shoes.'

Questioner: I would probably say, 'I don't want to put on my shoes!'

KRISHNAMURTI: Find out why I am asking you to. There are two people concerned, aren't there – you and I. I am asking you to put on your shoes. Why? Either I am conventional, or I want to boss you, or I see your feet are dirty, you'll dirty the carpet, or because it doesn't look nice to have dirty feet. I want to see that you understand what I am talking about.

Questioner: Shouldn't you tell me, then?

KRISHNAMURTI: Yes, that's why I am telling you. I'm not telling you because I'm orthodox, you follow? I explain all this to you and you resist and say, 'Why not? I did it at home, why not here?' Because here it's a different country, a different climate. And the crowd round about you, the neighbours, say: 'What's the matter with all those people there, going about half naked?' You set up a bad reputation. You see all that is involved in it. So you have to learn about all this, which does not mean that you conform to the bourgeois.

Questioner: I don't understand. If you're worried about what the others think, the others on the outside . . .

KRISHNAMURTI: I'm not worried. I'm living in the world.

73

If the outside people give this place a bad reputation, what happens?

Questioner: Trouble, probably.

KRISHNAMURTI: That's it. You will soon have to close the place. There are nasty people in the world.

Questioner: And then there will not be the security which we need.

KRISHNAMURTI: That's just it. So *learn* about it! Don't say: 'Why shouldn't I do what I like, to hell with the outside world, they're stupid.' I have to learn, I have to live in the stupid world.

To come back to the point. How are we, each one of us, going to make this our home? It's *your* job! Home means where you have energy, where you are creative, where you are happy, where you are active, where you are alive and not just learning from some book or other.

I have been travelling, talking, for the last fifty years. I go from country to country, from a room to a different room, different food, different climate. Wherever I am that little room is my home. You understand? I'm at home, I feel completely safe because I have no resistance.

So how are you going to make this place into your home from today? If you don't, will you allow someone to tell you that you don't? If I come along and say, 'Look, you are not making this into your home', will you listen to me then? Or will you say: 'What do you mean? It is my home, I interpret "home" in a different way from you.' You interpret the idea of home in one way and I interpret it in another way and we quarrel. Then it's not a home! The interpretation of an idea of what you consider to be a home does not bring about a home, but to have the real feeling of it – and that implies a certain yielding. Which doesn't mean that you accept authority.

If someone wants to come here who says, 'These are all a lot of rather immature children' (Sorry, but you *are*), 'What's going on here?' – and he is a disturbing factor –

74

how will you deal with him? Will you all say: 'Let's vote for him. We like his face, his appearance, or whatever it is, and therefore we all agree that he should come'? Is that the reason you are going to accept him? He may be a drunkard; he may do all kinds of things. How will you act? These are the problems which you are going to have to face in life. Do you understand? How are you going to meet it all? Thank God I have no children – but I feel this very strongly here. You are going to leave this place and be thrown to the wolves and you are not capable of meeting all this. You think you are all very clever – but you're not.

So, how can we live here wisely, with care and affection, so that when you go out into the world you are prepared for the monstrous things that are happening? How will you bring about order in this house? Do please consider this seriously. As you pass by a room, if you see everything lying on the floor – what will you do?

Questioner: Pick it up.

KRISHNAMURTI: And do that every day? *(Laughter.)*

Questioner: You ask him to put his things away.

KRISHNAMURTI: And he doesn't!

Questioner: Tell him why he should. Remind him.

KRISHNAMURTI: All right. You remind me ten times!

Questioner: You tell him why.

KRISHNAMURTI: Yes, you tell me all that but I'm sleepy. I don't care. I don't learn. I'm dull-witted. What are you going to do? Beat me up? And I consider it's my home too, as well as yours. What are you going to do with me?

You don't answer! It is your home, and if you have a room in disorder some part of the house is being destroyed. It's like setting fire to a house. What will you do?

Questioner: Put it out!

75

KRISHNAMURTI: You put it out every day and he lights it every day? Find out. Don't give it up. It's your life! *(Pause.)* What do you say, what do you do? It's your home and I dirty the floor every day. How are you going to deal with me?

Questioner: The problem is that somebody cares about it and somebody else doesn't care about it.

KRISHNAMURTI: What will you do?

Questioner: Find out why.

KRISHNAMURTI: Yes. And I'll tell you all the reasons! You see, you're missing the point. I keep my room in disorder; there is dirt on the carpet, I dirty everything. What will you do with me? You have told me ten times and I go on doing it.

Questioner: If there is no communication . . .

KRISHNAMURTI: What are you going to *do*? Don't say 'no communication'. You are all finding excuses. Let's put it another way. You are responsible, you are the Principal . . . what are you going to do?

Questioner: It's as you say. If there is dirt and it's like a fire, there is no end to it. Either you say, ' You are part of this home, you should take care of it' or, ' You can't destroy the home'.

KRISHNAMURTI: So what are you going to do with me?

Questioner: Well, if you feel it's your home you'll do it, won't you?

KRISHNAMURTI: Then, why don't I?

Questioner: (Many interjections.)

KRISHNAMURTI: Go into it. You will see. The moment I come here it's your responsibility to see that I understand what it means to feel at home. Not after making an awful mess of it. Perhaps you and I feel at home. But make the third person feel at home, then you will have order. But if you don't care and I don't care, then the other person says, 'All right, I'll do as I like.'

So all of us are going to bring about this feeling that it is our home. Not Mrs Simmons going round putting everything in order and telling us what to do and what not to do. We are all doing it together. Do you know what vitality it will give you? What energy you will have? Because now the energy is wasted in sentimental emotionalism and conflicts. When we feel that this is our home we will have tremendous vitality.

Questioner: Well, everybody comes from different backgrounds, and therefore it is . . .

KRISHNAMURTI: Quite right. But they all want one thing: security.

Questioner: Yes, but it's just their own form of security.

KRISHNAMURTI: Ah no – not *your* form of security and *my* form of security, but the *feeling* in which there is no fear. A feeling of being completely together. A sense of, 'I can trust you', 'I can tell you anything about myself.' It's not my telling you in my own way or having particular idiosyncrasies, but I feel at home, I feel a sense of complete protection. Don't you know what it all means? Probably you don't feel this at home when you go back?

Questioner: Well, when you go home you feel at home. I think I do. But I don't keep my room that neat. When I come here, I don't know why I should be so neat here.

KRISHNAMURTI: It's not a question of neatness. First, it's the feeling. As we have said, one functions better when one feels completely safe, and most of us don't feel safe anywhere because we build a wall of resistance round ourselves, we have isolated ourselves. In that isolation we may feel safe, but that isolation can be broken into at any time. Now, is there the feeling of having no resistance? I don't know if you understand this? When we are really friends, when I love you and you love me – not sex and all that – but really feeling together, then we are safe, aren't we? You will protect me and I will protect you in the sense of working together, but not in the sense of resisting others. Now, can't we live like this? Can't we create that feeling here? Otherwise, what's the point of all this? Can't we have a sense of wellbeing, a sense of caring, of affection, love? Surely, then we shall create something totally new!

Look what happens. A mother brings up a baby. Think of the care – months and months of getting up at two o'clock at night; and then as the children grow up they are pushed out. Society swallows them up and sends them to Vietnam or somewhere else. And here there is this sense of being so safe. And *you* have to create it because it's your home, your furniture, your books, your food, your carpet. You understand?

I know a man who said to his daughter: 'You are going to get married and I know what that means. You will always be in trouble, you will be in strife with your husband and all the rest of it. But here you always have a room. It's your home.' Do you know what happened? There was tremendous trouble between husband and wife. But she used to come to this room and become quiet, rest, and be happy in it, even if only for a little while. I used to know the family fairly well.

Questioner: But in the story the girl is only being quiet, resting in the room.

KRISHNAMURTI: Yes, but you can see the implication for this place.

Questioner: When one has accomplished this feeling of being at home, one is at home anywhere.

KRISHNAMURTI: Then begin here. Then you will be at home anywhere.

Questioner: And you don't just 'accomplish' it. You go on ac-complishing it.

KRISHNAMURTI: But if you don't know what the feeling is now, when you are young, and don't create it, then later on it is too late.

Do you know anything about meditation? You are inter-ested in sex, aren't you? You are interested in being enter-tained; you are interested in learning geography, history – interested casually. You are interested in many things, aren't you? Meditation is part of life; don't say it's some-thing outside for some silly people. It's part of existence, so you must know about it as you must know about mathe-matics, electronics or whatever it is. Do you know what it means to meditate? The dictionary meaning of the word is 'to ponder', 'to think over', 'to ruminate', 'to enquire into'. Shall we talk a little about it?

When you sit very quietly, or lie down very quietly, the body is completely relaxed, isn't it? Have you ever tried to sit very, very quietly? Not to force it, because the moment you force it, it is finished. To sit very quietly, either with your eyes closed or open. If you have your eyes open there is a little more distraction, you begin to see things. So, after looking at things, the curve of the tree, the leaves, the bushes, after looking at it all with care, then close your eyes. Then you will not say to yourself, 'What's happening, let me look.' First *look* at everything – the furniture, the colour of the chair, the colour of the sweater, look at the shape of the tree. After having looked, the desire to look out is less. I've seen that blue sky and I've finished with it and I won't look again. But you must first look. Then you can sit quietly. When you sit quietly, or lie down very quietly, the blood flows easily into your head, doesn't it? There is no strain. That's why they say you must sit cross-legged with head very straight, because the blood flows easier that way. If you sit crouched it is more difficult for the blood to go into the head. So you sit or lie down very, very quietly. Don't force it, don't fidget. If you fidget, then watch it, don't say, 'I must not.' Then, when you sit very quietly, you watch your mind. First, you watch the mind. Don't correct it. Don't say, 'This thought is good, that thought is not good' – just watch it. Then you will see that there is a watcher and the watched. There is a division. The moment there is a division there is conflict.

Now, can you watch without the watcher? Is there a watching without the watcher? It is the watcher that says, 'This is good and that is bad', 'This I like and that I don't like' or, 'I wish she hadn't said this or that', 'I wish I had more food'.

To watch without the watcher – try it some time. That's part of meditation. Just begin with that. That's good enough. And you will see, if you have done it, what an extraordinary thing takes place . . . your body becomes very, very intelligent. Now the body is not intelligent because we have spoiled it. You understand what I mean? We have destroyed the natural intelligence of the body itself. Then you will find that the body says: 'Go to bed at the right time.' It wants it, it has its own intelligence and activity. And also if it wants to be lazy, let it be lazy.

Oh, you don't know what all this means! You try it. When I come back in April we'll sit down together twice a week and go into all this, shall we? Good! I feel you ought to leave this place highly intelligent. Not just pass some exams, but be tremendously intelligent, aware, beautiful persons. At least that is how I feel for you.

6

Three kinds of energy. Conflict and wastage of energy. Action without conflict. The early morning meeting.

KRISHNAMURTI: Has one got creative energy and how can one release it? You know what I mean by that? We've got plenty of energy when we want to do something. When we want to do it very badly, we've got enough energy to do it. When we want to play or go for a long walk we have energy. When we want to hurt people, we have energy. When we get angry, that's an indication of energy. When we talk endlessly, that's also an expression of energy.

Now what is the difference between this and creative energy? Does this interest you?

Questioner: Yes.

KRISHNAMURTI: What is the difference – I'm just thinking aloud now – what is the difference between physical energy, and energy that is brought about through friction, such as anger, tension, dislike. There is purely physical energy, and there is the energy derived through tension, through conflict, through ambition. And is there any other kind of energy?

We only know these two. The energy that a good, healthy body has – tremendous energy. And the energy that one gets through every kind of struggle, friction, conflict. Have you noticed this? The great writers who lead terrible lives, miserable lives of conflict in their relationship with others and with people generally: this tension gives them a tremendous energy. And because they've got a certain capacity, a gift to write, that energy expresses itself through writing. You see all this?

Now what kind of energy have you? Physical energy –
naturally, being young, you should have plenty of it, an
abundance of it. And have you the other kind of energy
which drives you, through hate, through anger, through
ambition, through tension, through conflict, resistance?
Because if I resist you I have tremendous energy. I dislike
you, I fight you, because I want to have your – whatever it
is – and that gives me energy. And behind that energy there
is a motive.

Now you see the two types: physical energy; and energy
which comes through conflict and resistance, through fear,
or the pursuit of pleasure. Is there any other kind of energy?
Is there energy which is without motive?

I want to get a job because I need it; and the drive for it,
the necessity for a job, this gives enough energy to ask,
demand, push, be aggressive. There is a motive behind it.
And where there is motive, the energy is always restricted,
limited. The moment there is a motive, it acts as a brake.
You see the point?

So have you that kind of energy that is always having a
brake put on it because it has a motive? Discuss with me!
I'm just thinking it out. Have you ever done anything without a motive? A motive such as fear, like and dislike, wanting something from someone, being as good as another:
those are all motives which drive one forward.

Now do you know any action without any motive? Is
there such action at all? We're enquiring. What do you say?

*Questioner: The problem being . . . whether you're conscious or not
of the motive – because you can have an action with a motive but if
you're . . .*

KRISHNAMURTI: Unconscious of it . . .

Questioner: . . . then you . . .

KRISHNAMURTI: Quite right. So you're saying, I may
think I am acting without a motive and yet have a motive
which is hidden.

Questioner: Yes; or the contrary.

KRISHNAMURTI: Or the contrary. Now which is it in yourself, enquire, go into yourself, find out? Look at yourself. Do you know what it is to look at yourself? Don't you look at yourself in the mirror when you comb your hair – you do, don't you? Now what do you see? You see your reflection in the mirror, exactly what you look like is reflected there, unless the mirror is crooked or cracked. Can you look at yourself in the same way as you see yourself in the mirror? Look at yourself without any distortion, without any twist, without any deviation, just to see exactly as you see yourself in a mirror. And only then you will find out whether you are acting with a motive or without a motive. Can you look at yourself very simply and very clearly, as though you were looking at yourself in a mirror? You know, it's very difficult, what we're talking about. I don't know whether you have ever done it; we're investigating into the question whether all our actions – going to meals punctually, getting up, whatever we do – have a motive behind them. Or is there a certain sense of freedom to move?

Questioner: What do you mean by freedom to move?

KRISHNAMURTI: Freedom just to move, without fear, without resistance, without a motive – to live. And to find that out! We're saying, you have enough physical energy – if you want to build a model aeroplane you build it. It would take time, you investigate, you enquire, you read about it, you put your mind and heart into it and build it. That requires a great deal of energy. The motive there is the interest to build. In that, is there any friction, any struggle, any resistance? You want to build that aeroplane. I come along and prevent you and say, 'Please, don't be silly, that's childish' – and you resist me, because your interest is to build. Now see what happens – when you resist me, you're wasting your energy, aren't you? And therefore you have less energy to build the aeroplane. Go into it, take time, watch it.

Now can your interest not be weakened, though I resist you, though I say you are silly? You see the point? I want to go out for a walk, for it's a lovely day. I want to see the trees, listen to the birds, see the new leaf, the marvellous spring day, I want to go out. And you come along and say, 'Please help me in the kitchen.' What takes place? I'm bored in the kitchen, I don't want to go because my interest is to go out for a walk. So there is a division in me, isn't there? The division is a waste of energy, isn't it? I want to go out for a walk so much and you come and ask me, 'Please help me in the kitchen.' Which shall I do?

Come on, I'm doing all the investigation, you just listen! What shall I do? Knowing that it's a wastage of energy if I say, 'Oh what a bore the kitchen is and I really want to go out for a walk.' What shall I do, so that I shall not waste energy? Come on, discuss with me. What shall I do?

Questioner: What do you mean by waste of energy?

KRISHNAMURTI: I'll show you. You ask me to come and help you in the kitchen. I really want to go out for a walk. If I am only doing what I want to do and go out for a walk, what happens to your question, 'Come and help me?' I have a feeling of guilt, don't I. 'All my walk is spoilt,' I say. 'Oh Lord, I ought to have gone,' – I fight. That's a wastage of energy, isn't it?

Questioner: You mean just the conflict.

KRISHNAMURTI: Conflict is a wastage of energy, isn't it? So what shall I do, knowing if I yield to you, if I come to the kitchen, I say, 'My God, what a lovely day it is, why am I not out.' And if I do go out for a walk I'll be saying, 'My goodness, I should be in the kitchen.'

Questioner: See what's needed more.

KRISHNAMURTI: No, not what is more needed. How would you answer this, so that I do something without wastage of energy, which is conflict. You've understood my

84

question, have you? Come on, Rachael, what shall I do? I don't want to have a struggle in myself. I shall have a struggle if I go out for a walk when you've asked me to come and help you. If I go into the kitchen and I really want to go out for a walk, I'll also have a struggle in myself. I want to do something without a struggle. What shall I do in these circumstances?

Questioner: Explain your feelings to the person who's asked you.

KRISHNAMURTI: Why should I explain?

Questioner: So the person will understand.

KRISHNAMURTI: Yes, he asked me to come and help him, he wants my help – too few people want to peel potatoes, so he asked my help. Can I talk to him and say, 'Look, I really want to go out for a walk, it's such a lovely day – do come with me.' But the potatoes have to be peeled. So what shall I do?

Questioner: Act responsibly, responsively.

KRISHNAMURTI: Act responsively, that is, act with responsibility, are you saying? Now what is my responsibility here – I'd love to go out for a walk, that's my responsibility too. So what shall I do?

Questioner: How does one know that the walk gives more pleasure than the kitchen?

KRISHNAMURTI: It's a beautiful day, lovely clouds and to go and peel potatoes is terrible when the birds are calling! So what shall I do? Use your brain-cells, come on!

Questioner: (1) It doesn't matter what you do as long as, after you've said that you're really not going to help in the kitchen, you go out for the walk – as long as you just leave it there.

Questioner: (2) You go to the kitchen and afterwards you go for the walk. (Laughter.)

KRISHNAMURTI: When I do go a walk, I'll be tortured by my conscience or whatever it is.

Questioner: But if you understand the whole situation would there be this conflict?

KRISHNAMURTI: What is the whole situation? The kitchen, the lovely sunlight and shade, and my desire to go out for a walk.

Questioner: This happened to me . . .

KRISHNAMURTI: This happens to all of us.

Questioner: The point being, whatever you do, you're going to be in conflict.

KRISHNAMURTI: No, I'm not going to be in conflict.

Questioner: If the kitchen really needs me, I'll go and help in the kitchen.

KRISHNAMURTI: He says he needs you, so you'll go there. But what happens to your walk?

Questioner: You go afterwards. The walk's always there . . .

KRISHNAMURTI: Wait – there are huge clouds and darkness comes. And I say, 'It's raining, why did you spoil my walk.'

Questioner: . . . you'd probably have got wet anyway. (Laughter.)

KRISHNAMURTI: What do you do, go into the kitchen? Or say, 'Go to hell, I'm going for a walk'?

Questioner: You act.

KRISHNAMURTI: What is your action based on?

Questioner: Just direct energy.

KRISHNAMURTI: You say you'll act – what is that action in which there is no conflict? Listen to it, what will you do in this situation when two things are contradictory – kitchen, walk? Have you got my question right?

Questioner: What is the thing that creates the conflict?

KRISHNAMURTI: The conflict is: the contradictory demands, the demand to go out for a walk and your demand for my help. I'm pulled in two directions. Now what shall I do so that there is only one direction in which there is no conflict. You understand the beauty of this question?

Questioner: When you see the urgency of helping in the kitchen . . .

KRISHNAMURTI: You see the urgency of the demand and you drop yours. Can you drop your desire, which is very strong, to go out for a walk, and comply to his demand, totally? Will you do that?

Questioner: When I see the urgency of his demand . . .

KRISHNAMURTI: Can you drop your urgency to go for a walk and accept his demand with grace, with ease, without any conflict?

Questioner: If you see the danger of the conflict.

KRISHNAMURTI: Do you see the danger of conflict, that it is poisonous, that it is a wastage of energy, that it doesn't lead anywhere? So can you drop your desire for a walk and just walk into the kitchen, equally happy, equally at ease, and forget your walk altogether? Because if you don't forget your walk, it's going to keep on nagging at you, isn't it?

Questioner: Surely everything is making these demands on us all the time, silently, verbally and non-verbally.

KRISHNAMURTI: Everything is based on this. That's what I'm getting at. I want to stay in bed and I have to be punctual for breakfast. You go into the kitchen with a grudge, don't you? So I am asking, can you do something contrary to your desire and· yet be in a state in which conflict doesn't exist. This is life, this is what happens all the time. Someone wants me to do something and I want to do something else. And then they begin to nag me and I resist.

Questioner: On the other hand, if you always yield . . .

KRISHNAMURTI: If I'm always yielding I become a doormat. So can I find out how to act when there are contradictory demands – an action in which there is no friction, there is no grudge, there is no resistance, no antagonism. Can you do this?

Questioner: It depends how strong the desire is.

KRISHNAMURTI: However strong, the mind *is* intense.

Questioner: I compare the two demands.

KRISHNAMURTI: No, not comparison.

Questioner: I mean, I want to do something, and somebody asks me to do something else – I have to compare those two.

KRISHNAMURTI: No, this is not comparison. You come and ask me to help you and I want to go out for a walk – I don't compare. There is no comparison between the two.

Questioner: I see comparison because . . .

KRISHNAMURTI: No, that comes when I say, 'Which is more important in this, my walk or going into the kitchen.' I say, 'The kitchen is more important.' What has taken place? I am evaluating and basing my action on what is important. But I don't want to base my action on what is important.

Questioner: But when the house catches fire . . . ?

KRISHNAMURTI: The house is on fire, the walk has gone – finished.

Questioner: Isn't this the same on a smaller scale, you evaluate what is at the moment necessary?

88

KRISHNAMURTI: No, I don't want to base my action on discrimination, on what is important.

Questioner: Why?

KRISHNAMURTI: I'll show you why. Who is the judge who says, this is important and that's not important? Myself, isn't it?

Questioner: It is the circumstances . . .

KRISHNAMURTI: You may consider that it's important and I might consider that it's not important, therefore there's friction between us. So I don't want to base my action on what is important.

Questioner: Isn't there an objective, not subjective, factor?

KRISHNAMURTI: Factually, not based on importance but fact. The fact is, he asks me to come into the kitchen and the fact is I want to go out for a walk.

Questioner: You still have to evaluate . . .

KRISHNAMURTI: Go into it slowly, carefully, it's quite interesting. Now, if I base my action on discrimination, what is important, what is not important, my discrimination may be the outcome of my prejudice, of my conditioning. So I say discrimination is very petty, because it's based on my conditioning, my prejudice, my opinion, my tendency. I won't base my action on discrimination. I won't base my action on evaluation.

Questioner: Evaluation of what I think. Isn't there still the evaluation that is not coloured by what I think?

KRISHNAMURTI: There is – I'm first clearing the ground. I will not discriminate, evaluate, because if I evaluate it might be based on my prejudice, my tendency, my wish, my imagination. So I won't base my action on my evaluation. Therefore I won't act on what is important and what is not important. I'm going to go into this – are you meeting me? This is a dangerous thing we are entering into – unless you understand very clearly you must stop me. Otherwise you'll pick up a few words and say, 'This is not important', and throw it at Mrs Simmons' head. So I've realized that if I evaluate it might be based on prejudice. But evaluation is necessary. When the teacher makes a report and says you are not good at French and very good at mathematics, that's evaluation, based on facts, not on your prejudice. Do you see the difference? You're a little bit suspicious?

Questioner: It's very difficult because . . .

KRISHNAMURTI: Say I'm teaching you Italian. I know much more Italian than you do, obviously, otherwise I wouldn't be teaching. And I see that you're not very good at Italian, factually, it's not my prejudice – after six months you don't know how to put a sentence together. That's a fact. On that fact I evaluate, not on my prejudice. Do you agree? That is entirely different from an evaluation about what is important.

Questioner: Is it evaluation whether you want tea or coffee?

KRISHNAMURTI: Don't reduce it to tea or coffee – just look at it first. So there are two factors in evaluation: prejudice and fact. When I evaluate what is important and what is not important it may be based on my prejudice and not on fact. And when he asks me to go into the kitchen, is it a fact or does he just want to annoy me? So I go in there and see what it is. If it's needed I do it and forget about it, because it's the fact that demands my action. You see the difference?

Questioner: I understand in this case . . .

KRISHNAMURTI: Understand this case and understand the general principle of it. If I evaluate what is important or not important, it is based perhaps on my prejudice, therefore I distrust my judgement in evaluation. But when facts demand evaluation, facts decide the value. The two are very clear, aren't they? Aren't they very clear?

Questioner: It's very clear when on one side you have your desires and on the other side you're needed. If on both sides you are needed, you have to choose either one or the other.

KRISHNAMURTI: No, I won't choose.

Questioner: You have to act – either one or the other.

KRISHNAMURTI: No, when you have to act, this or that, that means choice, and that means you don't know what to do and you choose which is more pleasurable.

Questioner: It's extremely difficult for a conditioned person to see truth without bias.

KRISHNAMURTI: Look, begin again. I want to go out for a walk and you come and ask me to go into the kitchen. If I ask what is more important, the kitchen or my walk, I evaluate according to my pleasure, according to my wish, my prejudice. Therefore I say to myself, 'I won't evaluate. The facts will produce the right action.' So I go with him into the kitchen and see if the fact demands it. The fact says, 'Yes,' and I forget the rest.

Questioner: Yes, but if you're needed in the kitchen at the same time as you're needed in the office?

KRISHNAMURTI: That's a different matter. The fact will tell me what to do. Then I realize, when the fact tells me what to do there is no friction. You see the beauty of it? Come on, you're not too young, are you? So the facts are the final factor of decision, of action, not my prejudice.

Questioner: If both are of equal . . .

KRISHNAMURTI: My prejudice and the fact are two different things. My desire, my pleasure, my wish, my longing, my tendency are entirely different from the fact of the kitchen. That makes your mind so clear, then there is no choice between the kitchen and your walk. The fact has decided that you go to the kitchen and that is the end of it. You know, that demands a great deal of intelligence. A man who says, 'I want to go for a walk and I'm going – who are you to call me into the kitchen, you're authoritarian, you're a bully' – to say that is a waste of time and energy. Much better to say, 'Go away, please, I'm going for a walk, ask somebody else.' That would be much simpler, wouldn't it? But we are frightened to say that. You know, I've described all this, but the words are not the fact.

Questioner: I would like to examine it from a different point of view.

KRISHNAMURTI: Go ahead.

Questioner: Take this case: I've been working on studies for six or seven hours. And then I feel the need to have a little break and have a walk. And some people say, 'Come into the kitchen and help.'

KRISHNAMURTI: What will you do?

Questioner: It's a fact that I took the break to have a rest.

KRISHNAMURTI: So what will you do?

Questioner: Even if I go into the kitchen, I won't pay full attention.

KRISHNAMURTI: So you ask, what is the fact – stick to facts.

Questioner: The fact is I'm tired.

KRISHNAMURTI: You're tired, that's good enough. 'Sorry, I'm tired, I can't come into the kitchen.' That's all. But be honest – not pretending to be tired.

So let's come back. There is physical energy and we have plenty of it, because we have good food, rest, and so on. Then there is psychological energy which is dissipated in conflict. And I say to myself, 'That's a waste of energy.' Though in psychological conflict tension is created and out of that tension grows a certain kind of energy. And if I have a capacity as a writer, as a speaker, or as a painter, I use that capacity, which is a wastage of psychological energy.

So can I act psychologically, without wastage of energy, based on facts only and nothing else. You understand what I am saying? Only facts and not psychological, emotional prejudice – 'I must, I must not.' Then you have harmony between the psyche and the physical. Then you have a harmonious way of living. From there you can find out if there is another kind of energy of a totally different kind. But without having the harmony between the psyche and the physical, psychosomatic harmony, then your enquiry into the other has no meaning.

Now, you have listened to this. What are you going to do with your life, what are you going to do this morning, or this afternoon, when this problem arises? It is going to arise, every day of your life it's going to arise: come into the kitchen, go out for a walk, build an aeroplane, or come for a drive. School, class, stay in bed, 'Oh, must I get up so early?'

So what will you do? What you will do depends on how you have listened. If you have really listened you will from now on just act on facts only – that's a marvellous thing, you don't know the beauty of it – just on facts. Instead of bringing all your emotional circus into it.

Did you find any difference after Sunday's talk about laziness? You remember we said, don't use the word 'lazy', but find out why you want to stay in bed longer. Have you gone into it? Rose, have you gone into that other question, which was, we are hurt, from childhood we are hurt, by our mothers, by our fathers, by our neighbours, by our friends – people hurt us. Now can you not be hurt any more? – which doesn't mean resist, which doesn't mean build a wall round yourself, but which means not to have an image about yourself. Have you an image about yourself?

Can you look at it all, not be so terribly attached to your

long hair, or short hair? We're always talking about long hair, short hair here – what a waste of time! You know what it is to be pliable? Have you ever watched a river? You have? How it flows over a rock, how it moves, never caught in a corner, in a little pool – moving, moving, moving. And if you don't at this age keep on moving, you're going to be caught in a little pool of your own making and that is not the river, that's dirty water. An image isn't merely a picture about something: a conclusion is an image, a conclusion that I am something, that I must be something – that's an image.

You know there is a school I go to in North India, just like this, but it's got three hundred acres and a marvellous river – the Ganges – it's on the banks of the Ganges, you see the river flowing by. It is really most extraordinary, that river. It comes down passing the big city called Benares, comes down. You see people washing their clothes, bodies being burnt and thrown into the river, people bathing, doing their laundry and another man drinking the water – all this is taking place within a few yards. And that river is always alive – because it's alive its water is not contaminated, is not polluted. Several doctors some years ago took that water to Switzerland to cure stomach troubles.

I was rowing once on that river and as I put my hand down to see how cold the water was, an arm was floating by. Because the tradition there in India, specially round Benares, is that your body must be burnt on the river bank – in India they cremate their bodies, they don't bury them – it's much simpler and it occupies less space.

So the poor people bring their dead relatives, come to the river bank, buy wood and with a little wood they burn the body. But they haven't the time to wait there till the body is consumed as they have to hurry back to their village. So the man who sells the wood puts the fire out, preserves the wood, throws the body into the river, and sells the wood to the next person who comes along. And you meet that body several miles below.

Questioner: Sir, I believe the water's been analysed and they found some extraordinary things.

KRISHNAMURTI: I know. The sacred river, that's why it's called sacred.

Questioner: We were discussing the morning meeting at our school meeting last night. There is some lack of clarity about it.

KRISHNAMURTI: With regard to what?

Questioner: The meeting before breakfast.

KRISHNAMURTI: What about it? Why do you meet?

Questioner: To be together.

KRISHNAMURTI: You're together all day. At the school I visit in Benares, they also meet every morning. At Rishi Valley they meet every morning and here you meet every morning – what for? You're against it, are you?

Questioner: No.

KRISHNAMURTI: Be simple. You're against it? No?

Questioner: Not against it, I don't like pressure from other people ...

KRISHNAMURTI: Wait, you don't like pressure being put on people – I'm putting pressure on you now by asking you what you think about it. You can tell me to go to hell, but people are putting pressure on you all the time, everybody is on somebody else – don't just say you don't like it. Your father is putting pressure on you, society is putting pressure on you, the books you read are putting pressure on you, the television, everything is putting pressure on you. You mean, 'I like to choose my pressures, the ones that are pleasurable.' That's all. So I'm asking you, do you like to meet in the morning? To come to a school is a pressure. So what do you say – you don't like it? Come on, be straight about these matters.

Questioner: Sometimes I like it.

KRISHNAMURTI: Now why do you meet at all? – I'm asking you.

Questioner: So that we hear different ideas and listen to everyone.

KRISHNAMURTI: That's right, that is, you want to listen to people, to the others. Is that the reason you meet?

Questioner: The reason could be different for different people.

KRISHNAMURTI: Why do you all meet?

Questioner: (1) To be quiet.

Questioner: (2) To be together.

KRISHNAMURTI: To listen to what others are saying, to be quiet, to be together – you've said three things. Is that the reason you meet?

Questioner: To make up an audience. (Laughter.)

KRISHNAMURTI: Why are you all sitting there?

Questioner: You're the speaker so we're the audience, we construct an audience to listen.

KRISHNAMURTI: Is that the reason you meet, because you are the audience? I'm asking, why do you meet here?

Questioner: (1) To discuss things together.

Questioner: (2) It's because during the day we don't pay attention to all the voices around us.

KRISHNAMURTI: You're saying we want to be quiet in the morning, to gather ourselves, to pay attention, to listen to people – to be together, to find out, to feel a sense of communal action together – is that why you come?

Questioner: (1) Because of habit.

KRISHNAMURTI: You go by habit?

Questioner: (2) No, I don't come here by habit.

KRISHNAMURTI: What is the point of being together in the morning? Isn't it important in the morning to be together, to sit quietly, to listen to the birds, to listen to a person who is reading a poem – do you read a poem? Oh, by the way, do you write poetry? Yes? I'm so glad, good. Is it good poetry? *(Laughter.)* In the mornings, shouldn't you meet together in the mornings to be quiet, sit together, to listen to what is being read, so that you collect yourself?

Questioner: So that everybody acts as one.

KRISHNAMURTI: No, not as one – I said gather yourself to be quiet.

Questioner: Wouldn't that mean, if you did that, that you were ungathered before you gathered yourself.

KRISHNAMURTI: But you are ungathered before.

Questioner: But why?

KRISHNAMURTI: Because you always happen to be that way. Are you gathered all the time? When you get up in the morning, what takes place? You rush, you do your bathing, toilet and all the rest of it, 'For God's sake, I've got ten minutes more left', and you rush through.

Questioner: No.

KRISHNAMURTI: No? But you are different. *(Laughter.)* We are orientals, we get up early, we do it more lazily. But some of you get up and rush and you keep rushing all day, don't you? No? That's just it, you rush all day, from class to class, meals, play, keep moving. So that there is no time for self awareness, for being quiet, to look at yourself, to look at the trees, look at the birds, hear their song, never a moment to be quiet. Shouldn't you have quietness? To be quiet does not mean to pick up a paper and look at it – but to be absolutely quiet. Isn't it necessary? Then is that quietness habit?

Questioner: No.

KRISHNAMURTI: No, you're not aware of your constant agitation during the day; therefore when you are aware that you are constantly moving, agitated, talking, reading – in the morning be quiet together. You know what happens if you're quiet that way?

Questioner: Why together? I mean you can be quiet on your own, too.

KRISHNAMURTI: Oh yes, I'm not saying you can't be quiet on your own, but when you're quiet together, it brings about a corporate action. Doesn't it? Haven't you noticed it? Then if somebody asked you to go into the kitchen, you'd go.

Questioner: But outside Brockwood we can't come together every morning in a group, or sit quietly.

KRISHNAMURTI: I said, to be together and to be quiet; then you read something and I listen, then you say something and I listen out of my quietness, not out of my agitation, you follow? I listen out of my quietness. Then I will really listen, then I will learn the art of listening, out of quietness. For that reason I would come to the meeting.

I went once to a monastery and stayed there a week. The monastery was run by some friends of mine in California. The programme was: you got up at six and bathed and all that. From 6.30 to 7.30 you sat in a darkened room, really dark; a man was in charge who read a passage from Brother Lawrence, the *Cloud of Unknowing*, or some philosophical or devotional book – he read for two or three minutes. Then for that whole hour you sat. It was a small amphitheatre – you know what an amphitheatre is – steps going down, and each person sat on a step with his feet down on the next. So you sat in the complete darkness for an hour and meditated. That was demanded of you.

Then from 7.30 to 8.0 you prepared the breakfast all together, and from 8.30 or a quarter to nine, you washed up all the dishes, and then went to your room to clean up and make the bed and so on. At 10.30 somebody gave a talk about whatever it was, science, philosophy, biology or anthropology. From 11.30 to 12.30 in that darkened room, meditation for an hour. Then lunch. After lunch you never said a word to anybody and then from 5.30 you went out for a walk or did something in the garden, or went to your room, but no talking. From 6.30 to 7.30 meditation in the dark room and dinner, washing dishes. From after lunch till the next morning after meditation you never talked. Now, if you followed that, it would be forming a habit, wouldn't it, because it was the custom, it was the thing to do? But unfortunately or fortunately that monastery broke up.

As a student or teacher here, I would go to a morning meeting because I wanted to sit quietly for a few minutes, or half an hour, not only to look and listen to what other people were saying, or what was being read, but also to look at myself. I want to see what kind of animal I am, what kind of person I am, why I do this and why I do that, why I think this, why I want that – I want to know myself. Because when I know myself, then I have great clarity, then I can think very clearly, very simply, very directly. I would do that in the morning meetings – read, listen, and also sit quietly to see what I am – see the beauty of what I am, or see the ugliness of what I am, just to see, to observe. And when I come out of that there's a delight in my eyes, because I've understood something.

7

On sitting quietly with a still mind.

Questioner: Could we talk about sensitivity and consideration for others?

KRISHNAMURTI: Man has always wanted something holy, sacred. Just being kind to others, being sensitive, polite, considerate, thoughtful and affectionate: that hasn't got depth, it hasn't got vitality. Unless you find out in your life something really sacred which has depth, which has tremendous beauty, which is the source of everything, life becomes very superficial. You may be happily married, with children, a house and money, you may be clever and famous, but without that perfume everything becomes like a shadow that has no substance.

Seeing what is happening around the world, will you, in your daily life, find out something that is really true, really beautiful, holy, sacred? If you have that, then politeness has meaning, then consideration has meaning, has depth. Then you can do anything you like, there will always be that perfume. How will you come to this? It is part of your education, not only to learn mathematics, but also to find this out.

You know, to see something very clearly – even that tree – your mind must be quiet, mustn't it? To see that picture I must look at it, but if my mind is chattering, saying 'I wish I were outside', or 'I wish I had a better pair of trousers', if my mind is wandering, I will never be able to see that picture clearly. To see something very clearly I must have a very quiet mind. See the logic of it first. To watch the birds, to watch the clouds, to watch the trees, the mind must be extraordinarily still to follow.

There are various systems in Japan and India to control

the mind so that it becomes completely quiet. And being very quiet you then experience something immeasurable – that is the idea. So they say: first the mind has to be quiet, control it, don't let it wander, because when you have a quiet mind life is extraordinary. Now when you control or force the mind you are distorting it, aren't you? If I force myself to be kind, that is not kindness. If I force myself to be extremely polite to you that is not politeness. So if I force my mind to concentrate on this one picture then there is so much strain, effort, pain and suppression. Therefore such a mind is not a quiet mind – you see? So we have to ask: is there a way of bringing about a very quiet mind without any distortion, without any effort, without saying, 'I must control it'?

Of course there is. There is a quietness, a stillness without any effort. That requires understanding of what effort is. And when you understand what effort, control, suppression is – understand it not just verbally but really see the truth of it – in that very perception the mind becomes quiet.

You meet every morning at eight o'clock. What takes place, what do you do when you meet?

Questioner: We sit quietly in the room.

KRISHNAMURTI: Why? Go on, discuss it with me. Do you read anything?

Questioner: Sometimes people read.

KRISHNAMURTI: What is the meaning of it? Why do you meet every morning?

Questioner: I have been told that it is to find a feeling of togetherness.

KRISHNAMURTI: Do you, sitting quietly, get a feeling of togetherness? Do you actually feel it? Or is this just an idea?

Questioner: Some do, some don't.

KRISHNAMURTI: Why do you meet at all? Come on, you don't discuss with me!

You know, meeting in the morning, sitting together, if you do it rightly it is an extraordinary thing. I don't know if you have ever gone into it. When you sit down, do you sit really quietly? Is your body really very quiet?

Questioner: No. It isn't quiet most of the time.

KRISHNAMURTI: Why isn't it quiet? Do you know what it means to sit quietly? Do you keep your eyes closed? Answer! I am doing all the talking. What do you do? Are you relaxed? Do you sit really quietly?

Questioner: Sometimes you are very relaxed.

KRISHNAMURTI: Wait, don't say 'sometimes'. This is only an escape, stick to one question.

Questioner: I am very quiet and very still.

KRISHNAMURTI: What do you mean by being quiet? Are you quiet physically?

Questioner: Yes.

KRISHNAMURTI: Which means what? Please listen to this. Are your nerves, your body movements and your eyes absolutely quiet? Is your body very quiet without twitching, without any movement and when you close your eyes are they still? To sit quietly means your whole body is relaxed, your nerves are not strained, not irritated, there is no movement in friction, you are physically absolutely quiet. You know, the eyes keep moving because you are always looking at things, therefore when you close your eyes keep them completely quiet.

You go into this room at eight o'clock in the morning to sit quietly so as to have harmony between your mind, your body and your heart. That is the beginning of the day, so that this quietness goes on throughout the day, not just for ten minutes or half an hour. That quietness goes on though you play games, shout or chatter, but at the core there is always the sense of this quiet movement – you follow?

Questioner: How?

KRISHNAMURTI: I am going to show you Do you see the importance of it? Don't ask 'How', first see the logic, the reason for it. When you meet in the morning for ten minutes you sit absolutely quietly, you may read something – it may be Shakespeare, or a poem – and you gather quietness.

Look, sit absolutely quietly without a single movement so that your hands, your eyes, everything are completely quiet – what happens? Somebody has read a poem and you have listened to it; while you were going to the room you watched the trees, the flowers, you have seen the beauty of the earth, the sky, the birds, the squirrels, you have watched everything around you. And when you have watched everything around you, you come into the room; then you don't want to look out any more. I wonder if you follow? You have finished with looking out (because later you will go back to it), you have finished by looking very carefully at everything as you came in. Then you sit absolutely quietly without a single movement; then you are gathering quietness without any forcing. Be quiet. Then when you leave, when you are teaching or when you are learning this or that, there is this quietness going on all the time.

Questioner: Isn't that a forced quietness?

KRISHNAMURTI: You didn't understand. You have had your bath, you come downstairs and you look, not just casually, but you *look* at the trees, you look at the bird going by, you look at the movement of the leaf in the wind. And when you do look, *look*. Don't just say 'I've seen that', but give your attention to it. Do you see what I am saying?

So before you come into the room look at everything clearly and with attention, with care. And when you come in and somebody reads something, you sit quietly. Do you see what happens? Because you have looked extensively at everything, then when you sit quietly, that quietness becomes natural and easy because you have given your attention to everything that you have looked at. You carry that attention over when you sit quietly, there is no wandering off, no wanting to look at something else. So with that attention you sit and that attention is quietness. You can't look if you are not attentive, which means being quiet. I don't know if you see the importance of this?

That quietness is necessary because a mind that is really very quiet, not distorted, understands something which is not distorted, which is really beyond the measure of thought. And that is the origin of everything.

You see, you can do this not only when you are sitting in the room but all the time, whilst you are eating, talking, playing games; there is always this sense of attention you have gathered at the beginning of the day. And as you do it, it penetrates more and more. *Do it!*

Questioner: Sir, isn't the attention that one gives more important than sitting down and being quiet?

KRISHNAMURTI: I said, there is the attention that you have given to watching the birds, the trees, the clouds. And then when you go into the room you are gathering that attention, intensifying it – you follow? And that goes on during the day even though you don't pay attention to it. Try it tomorrow morning, I am going to question you about it. An examination! *(Laughter.)* Because when you leave this place you must have captured something – neither Hindu nor Christian – then your life will be sacred. *(Pause.)*
What do you say, Sophia? I am going to make her talk!

Questioner: At times we forget and in that time thought re-forms us all again.

KRISHNAMURTI: What you are saying is: I watched the birds, the trees, the leaf, the movement of the branch in the wind, I watched the light on the grass, the dew – I paid attention. And when I come into this room I am still attentive. Not attentive *to* anything – you follow? *There* I have been attentive to the bird, to the leaf. *Here*, when I come in, I am not attentive to anything – I am just attentive. Then in that state of attention thought comes in – doesn't it? 'I haven't done my bed', 'I must clean my shoes' or whatever it is and you pursue that thought. Go to the very end of that thought, don't say, 'I mustn't think that'. Finish it. In the process of finishing that thought a new thought arises. So pursue every thought to the very end, therefore there is no control, no restraint. It doesn't matter if I have a hundred thoughts. I am going after one thought at a time so that the mind becomes very orderly. I don't know if you are following all this?

Questioner: Where does silence come in then?

KRISHNAMURTI: You don't bother about silence because if thought is coming in you are not silent. Then don't force yourself to be quiet, pursue that thought.

Questioner: Is there any end to that?

KRISHNAMURTI: Yes, if you finish it; but if you don't go to the very end of it, it will come back because you haven't finished one thing. You have understood?

Look, I come out of the house, go round the lawn and watch, pay attention to the beauty, the tenderness, the movement of the leaf. I watch everything and I come into the room and sit. You read something and I sit quietly. I am trying to sit quietly and my body jerks because I have a habit of twitching, so I have to watch that, I pay attention to it, I don't correct it. You can't correct the movement of the leaf, can you? So in the same way I don't want to correct the movement of my hands, I watch it, I pay attention to it. When you pay attention to it, it becomes quiet – try it. I sit quietly, one second, two seconds, ten seconds, then suddenly up pops a thought: 'I have to go to some place this afternoon. I didn't do my exercises, I didn't clean the bath.' Or sometimes the thought is much more complicated: I am envious of that man. Now I feel that envy. So go to the very end of that and look at it. Envy implies comparison, competition, imitation. Do I want to imitate? – you follow? Go to the very end of that thought and finish it, don't carry it over. And when another thought pops up, you say, 'Wait, I'll come back to that.'

If you want to play this game very carefully, you write every thought you have on a piece of paper and you will soon find out how thought can be orderly because you are finishing every thought, one after the other. And when you sit quietly the next day you are really quiet. No thought pops up because you have finished with it; which means you have polished your shoes, you have cleaned your bath tub, you have put the towel in its right place at the right moment. You don't say when you sit down, 'I didn't put the towel back.' So the thing that you are doing is finished each time, and when you sit quietly you are marvellously quiet, you bring an extraordinary sense of orderliness into your life. If you haven't that orderliness you cannot be silent, and when you have it, when the mind is really quiet, then there is real beauty and the mystery of things begins. That is real religion.

8

The sense of beauty.

Questioner: There is something I'd like to discuss. I see that like and dislike are a matter of opinion – as what is ugly and what is beautiful – everyone has their own ideas. If I have no image about things, is there anything beautiful or ugly?

KRISHNAMURTI: To like: has that anything to do with affection, with love?

Questioner: No.

KRISHNAMURTI: Don't say, no or yes, go into it. And the feeling of beauty, does it come out of an image? Look at it – don't answer. I see a building created in space, and I say, 'How beautiful that is.' Now that expression, 'How beautiful', is it born of an image? Or is there no image, but the perception of something which has proportion, depth, quality, workmanship.

Questioner: You have an image of what is beautiful or of what you like: you are comparing it with something else. Your conditioning comes in.

KRISHNAMURTI: That's right. Watch it, it is much more complex than that. You see that tree – do you say it is beautiful? Why do you say it is beautiful, who has told you? Or, apart from the images, do you feel from everything a sense of beauty? – not related to trees, buildings, people. You understand? – *the sense of beauty* – not looking at anything particular.

Questioner: If you really look, it doesn't only happen with trees.

KRISHNAMURTI: You see a building and you say, 'How beautiful that is.' Is it because you have compared it with other buildings? – or because it is a famous building by Wren or the Ancient Greeks and so you say, 'What a marvellous thing that is.' Because you have been told about it and there is the image you have made about the man who built it; and so you comply because the popular thing to say is, 'How beautiful!' Or do you have a sense of beauty irrespective of anything created or not created? Have you understood my question?

Questioner: The sense of beauty has nothing to do with what you see.

KRISHNAMURTI: That's just it. The sense of beauty has nothing to do with what you see outside. Now what is that sense of beauty?

Questioner: A state of harmony.

KRISHNAMURTI: You are too quick in answering, go into it. What is that sense of beauty?

Questioner: It's vitality.

KRISHNAMURTI: It is a little more complex, go into it. As we said just now, if you have an image either about yourself, or an artist, or a great man, then that image is going to dictate what is beautiful, depending on the culture, on the popularity of the artist, or the statue, or the painting, this or that. So the image you have prevents the sense of beauty, in which there is no image.

Questioner: It prevents the very seeing.

KRISHNAMURTI: Of course. So, not to have images at all! You follow? – the image is the 'me'. When there is no 'me', there is the sense of beauty. Have you the sense of the 'me'? Then, when you say, 'That is beautiful', you are just re-acting to the image you have about what is beautiful, which is based on your literature, on your culture, the pictures, the museums to which you have been exposed. You can't ever say, 'How ugly!' when looking at a painting by Leonardo da Vinci; or when you are listening to Mozart, 'What a noise!' It is really quite extraordinary: to have no image about oneself is to have this sense of extraordinary beauty.

Questioner: If you listen to some music for the first time and you don't like it, through repetition you suddenly, or gradually, come to like it.

KRISHNAMURTI: Yes, what happens? You don't like Indian music, and you listen to it three or four times; then you begin to see something in it – not because you have been told – you listen. That means you are paying attention.

Questioner: You were paying attention the first time.

KRISHNAMURTI: The first time it was noise.

Questioner: You already have a notion what Western music is.

KRISHNAMURTI: You are used to Western music and you are suddenly faced with Chinese music. The first time you couldn't listen to it very carefully, there was a reaction – you follow? That is why any image, outer or inner, is the emphasis of the 'me', 'the ego', the personality, all that; and that absolutely prevents the quality and the sense of beauty. Which means, passion is not dependent nor the cause of something.

Questioner: If my sense of beauty makes me feel there is no difference between the beauty of the sun or the beauty of a tree . . . ?

KRISHNAMURTI: Wait, I have no image, therefore I have the sense of beauty, the feeling of beauty. And I see squalor, dirt, filth. I see a piece of paper on the road. What happens? I pick it up. When I see filth on the road I do something; socially, I act. I don't say, 'I have a sense of beauty, I don't see that.'

Questioner: I understand that. My sense of beauty is not destroyed by whatever goes on. Even if I close my eyes, it is not dependent on seeing.

KRISHNAMURTI: Absolutely right. But the sense of that beauty which is yours is mine also. It is not *my* sense of beauty or *your* sense of beauty, or the collective sense. It is beauty, the sense of beauty. To go into this is something passionate. It beats all books! But I mustn't say that, because you must pass exams!

9

What is it that wants to fulfil? What is 'myself'? What in me gets hurt? Walls of resistance. Learning about attention, awareness and sensitivity. Learning about image-making.

Questioner: Can we talk about reaction and how the moment we are reacting we don't see that we are reacting, only afterwards?

KRISHNAMURTI: Do you all want to discuss that? I think we can include that if we could discuss something with wider scope. We all want to fulfil, don't we?

Questioner: What do you mean by fulfil?

KRISHNAMURTI: Don't you feel that you would like to express yourself in different ways? – either writing a poem, or wearing a certain type of dress, or you want to become something in life.

Questioner: In fact, when you talk about it you see through it, but it's deeper than that.

KRISHNAMURTI: We're going to go into it more deeply. A woman feels that she is not fulfilled if she does not have a baby. A man feels frustrated if he does not work, if he does not do something in life. If you want to become something and are not able to, you feel frustrated, don't you? – you feel thwarted. What is it that wants to fulfil? What is behind that desire to fulfil? Who is it that is fulfilling?

Questioner: It can be an idea, for instance.

KRISHNAMURTI: I don't know, let's find out. If you say, 'This is my way of dressing, this is my way of acting, I want to express myself', what is this thing that wants to express itself? When I say 'myself', what is that?

Questioner: Isn't that an image of oneself?

KRISHNAMURTI: I don't know what you mean by that – find out. Don't you feel this? Or am I talking about something irrelevant? What do you say?

Questioner: At the moment I don't have a particular way of saying, 'This is my way of doing anything.'

KRISHNAMURTI: What do you mean 'my'? What do you mean by, 'It is my personal expression'? What is the thing behind it, the 'me' the 'self' that says, 'I must express myself, I must fulfil'?

Questioner: (1) Your ego?

Questioner: (2) It can be a reaction to feeling insecure.

KRISHNAMURTI: Yes.

Questioner: (1) And that's why it comes about, the feeling, 'That's my way.'

Questioner: (2) Isn't it a question not so much of 'my' way or 'your' way, but of finding out if there is a way which isn't influenced by 'you' or by 'me'?

KRISHNAMURTI: Which can only happen if I understand what is this 'me' that is always projecting itself, thrusting itself forward. What is that? 'My opinion, my judgement, my way of dressing, my way of keeping order' – what is that 'me'? Are you learning about that 'me'? Do you want to find out what that 'me' is? There are two different things: to learn about the 'me', and to find out if there is a 'me' at all.

Questioner: To learn about the 'me' first you have to make the 'me' exist.

KRISHNAMURTI: That's right, to learn about it. You see the difference?

Questioner: What do you mean, you have to make the 'me' exist?

KRISHNAMURTI: When I said there is a 'me', I've already stabilized it.

Questioner: (1) The purpose is to learn about it.

Questioner: (2) I know that it's there.

KRISHNAMURTI: Which means that I have a feeling it is there; all I have to do is to learn about it – its expressions, its way of acting, its resistances, its appetites and so on.

Questioner: One feels that this is the situation one is in, that one feels the 'me' does exist. Although I can say verbally that by saying this I am setting up the image of 'me', deeply within the feeling seems to make this 'me' there, so perhaps I can watch those feelings.

KRISHNAMURTI: We are trying to find out if there is a 'me', a 'self' which has to be studied. Or is there no 'me' and therefore, when I say 'I want to express myself,' what does that mean? Don't you feel the 'me' is important? What is that 'me' which says, 'I must fulfil, I must become, I must be this, that's my taste, I can go my way'?

Questioner: Is it something I cling to?

KRISHNAMURTI: You understand, Sarah, that when you say 'me' you have already established it, haven't you? And you resist anything that opposes that.

Questioner: Why? Why should we resist?

KRISHNAMURTI: I have established 'me' first. 'I' am this, 'I' am my prejudice, 'I' want to dress in a particular way, 'I' think this is the right way to have a tidy room.

Questioner: It's been drummed into us in childhood.

KRISHNAMURTI: That is the 'me' that must express itself, otherwise it feels thwarted. No? If I say, 'Look, Sarah, I don't like the way you dress', you will tell me that is the way you want to express yourself, that is your order. Now before you state, 'This is my order, my way of dressing,' what is

113

that 'me'? Have you established the 'me' that wants to express itself?

Questioner: What is the 'me' that says, 'You don't like the way I dress'?

KRISHNAMURTI: If I said to you I don't like the way you dress, what does that mean?

Questioner: It means you are expressing an opinion.

KRISHNAMURTI: Am I prejudiced? What is it that says, 'I don't like the way you dress'? And you reply, 'That's my taste.' There are two opposing statements. Who is it in you that says that's the way you want to dress? And who is the 'me' that says, 'That is not the way to dress'? Let's find out. Is it because I have a concept, an image, that mini-skirts are much better? And you say, 'I don't like them', you having your own idea of a long dress; and you say, 'That's the way to dress.' We have to live together in the same house, we come into contact. What do we do?

Questioner: I cling to the ideas which I have ...

KRISHNAMURTI: Don't theorize, then we are lost. See actually what the facts are, then we can deal with it. If you are speculating about it, then your speculation is as good as mine. What are these two: your 'I' and my 'I'?

Questioner: We both have a bundle of memories and experiences, we have developed certain preferences.

KRISHNAMURTI: That 'me' and that 'you' who assert themselves, are they prejudiced?

Questioner: Yes.

KRISHNAMURTI: Why do you say they are prejudiced?

Questioner: Let's investigate it.

KRISHNAMURTI: Let's probe into it. Do I react to my conditioning and you to your conditioning? You like long dresses and I don't like them, or whatever it is.

Questioner: The way you dress is an expression of your conditioning.

KRISHNAMURTI: Is it my prejudice or is it yours? Two prejudices coming into contact with each other explode – they have to do something. Why do I give such importance to the way you dress? And why do you resist what I say? Why don't you say, 'What does it matter'? Why don't we do this? Why this resistance?

Questioner: I think part of the resistance is to the way it is pointed out.

KRISHNAMURTI: I may point it out crudely, or I may point it out more gently, but why do you resist?

Questioner: Because if somebody hits you in a forceful way, then you react automatically. But if they say, 'Look, let's go into it, see why you dress the way you do,' then you discuss it, as we are doing now.

KRISHNAMURTI: We are doing it – but at the end of it, let's wipe it out, not just theorize day after day and talk about clothes – who cares!

Questioner: Didn't we make a distinction the other day between prejudice and preference? You said the other day . . .

KRISHNAMURTI: I don't care what I said the other day – you have to find out. It's not important what I said – what do *you* say? I'm asking you, Sarah, please tell me when I say this about your dress – is it a prejudice on my part? And when you say, 'This is my way of dressing,' is that your prejudice?

Questioner: Yes.

KRISHNAMURTI: Now what do you mean by prejudice – don't repeat what I said.

Questioner: When you have an idea about something and you're not willing to change it.

KRISHNAMURTI: Why aren't you willing to change it? Who is the person who asserts this?

Questioner: It's my 'me'.

KRISHNAMURTI: What is that 'me'?

Questioner: (1) It's part of myself, my conditioning, it's something I depend upon because without it, what am I?

Questioner: (2) Are you something?

KRISHNAMURTI: Isn't it part of your education to understand yourself?

Questioner: You asked if we care — but we do care, and I think it's very important . . .

KRISHNAMURTI: I am sorry. You all apparently do care tremendously about the way you dress.

Questioner: But why shouldn't we?

KRISHNAMURTI: I'm not saying you shouldn't. You do care, you give it a certain importance, that's all. Now what is the problem?

Questioner: The problem seems to me that we have to learn how not to react even if someone is prejudiced. We can't perhaps do very much about this prejudice, but supposing you say to me, 'I don't like the way you dress', you may or may not be prejudiced. But that is not what I have to go into, it's what I do about it.

KRISHNAMURTI: What will you do? We live in the same house.

Questioner: If I don't understand deeply why I shouldn't dress that way, if I just change, then it's hypocritical.

KRISHNAMURTI: Yes.

Questioner: And I don't want to be hypocritical. So it seems I am left with nothing to do.

KRISHNAMURTI: Why do we have such strong opinions about such trivial things?

Questioner: (1) I don't think it's the dress that bothers us – it's being hypocritical and taking somebody else's ideas or opinions for our own.

Questioner: (2) Why do you have an opinion anyway? It's me versus your opinion.

KRISHNAMURTI: Go on, Jimmy, help us out – don't just all sit quietly! She says, 'I don't want to be hypocritical,' that is, say one thing and do another.

Questioner: (1) But why is there the need to be hypocritical?

Questioner: (2) We have to be sensitive to the changing situation, but there is no set code, no set style of dress.

Questioner: (3) But your sensitivity is not the same as somebody else's.

Questioner: (4) It's not my sensitivity or your sensitivity, there is such a thing as sensitivity.

Questioner: (5) That's what we're trying to find out, is there such a thing and how can you get to that thing?

KRISHNAMURTI: Is that your problem?

Questioner: Yes, yes.

KRISHNAMURTI: How to be sensitive, not to any particular problem or to your own particular desires, but to be sensitive all around. What prevents you from being sensitive? – sensitive to my feelings, to somebody else's feelings, somebody's ideas, opinions, prejudices.

Questioner: This is not an objective situation, we all have a different idea of what to wear, you couldn't be equally sensitive to all the ideas . . .

KRISHNAMURTI: So you have to be sensitive all round, objectively and inwardly. Why aren't you? Is it because you don't want to be hurt, therefore you'll resist, you'll build a wall round yourself and at the same time say, 'I want to be sensitive.' Is that it?

Questioner: It's more a question of wanting to be able to function.

KRISHNAMURTI: You can function very well if you are extremely sensitive. That's the only way to function. You are very quick then, adjusting, not saying, 'This is right, I'm going to stick to it.' To every situation you are adjusting quickly – that's part of sensitivity, isn't it? Not your sensitivity, as she points out, or my sensitivity, which is absurd.

Questioner: Also, isn't there a larger dimension to the sensitivity? In other words, I can be sensitive to what you say, but there's a larger thing.

KRISHNAMURTI: Of course, that's what I'm implying.

Questioner: We live in a certain place and time and so forth, it wouldn't be appropriate to wear a suit of armour. There's a lot to be sensitive to. We tend to be sensitive about ourselves and to nothing else.

KRISHNAMURTI: Let's include all that. Why aren't we sensitive? What is preventing us from being sensitive all round? – to you, to me, objectively and subjectively.

Questioner: It is preventing us getting to know each other.

KRISHNAMURTI: He said that the fear of being hurt makes us insensitive, so we withdraw. Is that one of the major reasons for insensitivity? You have established the image of yourself which says, 'I must dress that way, it doesn't matter what the situation is, because I'm used to that way.'

Questioner: We're so concerned with our place in the whole that we don't look at the whole at all.

KRISHNAMURTI: That's it. Are you afraid of being hurt? Now what is the thing that is going to be hurt? Why don't you want to be hurt, what is it that fears being hurt?

Questioner: The ego, the self.

KRISHNAMURTI: The ego? What is that ego? What is it that says – 'I don't want to be hurt.'

Questioner: It's all your past.

KRISHNAMURTI: Go step by step, otherwise you'll miss it. When you say, 'I don't want to be hurt,' why are you saying that? Because you've already been hurt? Is that it? You've felt the pain of it and you say, 'I don't want to be hurt again.' You shrink back, you have been hurt in childhood and you say, 'I don't want to be hurt.' Now when you say that, it means – doesn't it? – that you've already been hurt, and you remember the past hurt and you don't want that to be repeated. Watch it: 'I don't want to be hurt.' 'I' being the memory of the past hurt, which says, 'I must be careful'. So what happens when you say, 'I don't want to be hurt'? What is the next step?

Questioner: You've got a resistance.

KRISHNAMURTI: You resist, don't you? Then what happens? Watch it, don't speak, see what happens. You build a wall round yourself in order not to be hurt. Then what happens?

Questioner: You get more hurt.

KRISHNAMURTI: I'm not going to help you with this. Go on, Jimmy. When I build a wall round myself in order not to be hurt, what takes place? You do the same and I do the same, each one is doing this. What happens?

Questioner: There is no communication.

KRISHNAMURTI: No communication? And you're trying to do things together, trying to co-operate, each building a wall around himself or herself. That is the basis of hypocrisy. When you say, 'I don't want to be a hypocrite', you are really saying, 'Leave me alone, don't hurt me.' You are sensitive in your way, I am sensitive in my way – which has no meaning.

Questioner: I want to understand, I don't just want to accept something I'm told.

KRISHNAMURTI: I see that I don't want to be hurt and I build a wall around myself, and you do the same – and as long as this wall exists there is no co-operation. I talk about co-operation and when I say to you, 'Please, this occasion doesn't demand that kind of dress,' you say, 'That's prejudice.'

Questioner: What is it in an occasion that dictates a specific dress?

KRISHNAMURTI: Leave the dress for the moment. You have a wall around yourself which is opinion, meaning, 'I am this, don't come beyond' – you are resisting because you don't want to be hurt. So you build a wall of opinion, of assertion, of aggression. You are not pliable, there is not a free play in it.

Questioner: (1) There are two things: the person who is expressing his own opinion, and there is an objective situation. Those two things get so mixed up. When you're saying the situation here is dictating something, it comes from what you're doing here, what you learn, how you behave.

Questioner: (2) How can you separate what is our own conditioned valuation of the situation and the actual situation. We haven't understood what the situation is here at Brockwood.

KRISHNAMURTI: Actually it's very simple. The situation is, each of us is protecting himself against the other, that's all. Right?

Questioner: I would say that's more important than all these other questions we've been raising.

KRISHNAMURTI: The other things are all so unimportant. When we understand this, everything else will fall into place. We have been raised in this modern world to do and think what we want. And we have developed this antagonism to anybody who says, 'This is different.'

Questioner: I don't think we have been raised to do what we want. I think ever since we've been growing up, people have said, 'Don't do this.'

KRISHNAMURTI: And then you resist that. And you break away from that and then you develop your own resistances. Behind all this – I'm just suggesting, I'm not saying it is so – there is this act of resistance; you in your way, I in my way, each person has the feeling, 'I must protect myself' – justly or unjustly. Then what shall we do? Living in a small community of this kind, if each one has a wall of resistance around him, how shall we work together? You know, this is an everlasting problem, not just here in Brockwood.

Questioner: Everybody will have to drop their defences which means they will have to drop what they think about particular things in order to look at them.

KRISHNAMURTI: Then what? I turn up in some absurd Indian clothes and you come and tell me, 'Don't dress that way, it's not suitable for this occasion!' And I resist you.

Questioner: But this is where there is a lot of energy wasted.

KRISHNAMURTI: I agree with you, it's a waste of energy.

Questioner: Sir, could we stay with the example you gave of absurd Indian dress. I can live with a person who wears Indian dress.

KRISHNAMURTI: Not that *you* can live with a person wearing absurd Indian dress, that's not the point. Am I incapable of being sensitive to the occasion which demands a different kind of dress?

Questioner: Let's look at why an occasion demands a certain dress.

KRISHNAMURTI: I'll show you. Have you seen Indian

ladies wearing saris? The other day in London I saw an Indian lady wearing a long sari, in India that's the fashion. She was sweeping the street with her sari, it was getting filthy, but she was totally unaware of it. What would you call that?

Questioner: It's appropriate to her.

KRISHNAMURTI: No, you don't get the point. She was totally unaware of what she was doing – that the long Indian dress was sweeping the street. She was unaware of it.

Questioner: But then, it's just as dirty in Bombay.

KRISHNAMURTI: *(Laughter.)* You are missing the point: *She* was totally unaware of it.

Questioner: Well, that's her problem.

KRISHNAMURTI: Please . . .

Questioner: Could I clarify whether the problem is that her dress was long and getting dirty, or whether it is the fact that she was wearing Indian dress in England?

KRISHNAMURTI: No, it's not that. I'm pointing out the insensitivity of a person who is unaware of what she is doing. That's all.

Questioner: But if you are sensitive to the situation . . .

KRISHNAMURTI: That's all I'm saying. My point is, if that Indian woman in London was aware of what she was doing, she would obviously lift up her sari.

Questioner: Because she wouldn't want to waste her energy washing it.

KRISHNAMURTI: Not only that, no, much more. The total unawareness of the occasion.

Questioner: It's a question of being asleep or being awake.

KRISHNAMURTI: Yes. It's not, 'Why do you care how she walks or what she does, it's her way of doing it,' as you said. I am asking, are you aware of what you are doing – not of the occasion, not of what you wear. But are you aware why you dress the way you do? Why do you feel it's of tremendous importance that you do things the way you do? That's the problem, isn't it?

Questioner: You seem to imply that once I'm aware of the way I'm dressing, I'll change.

KRISHNAMURTI: No, I did not say that. You may or may not change, it's up to you. But I am suggesting – are you aware of it? And being aware, see all the implications – not just being aware that you've got trousers on. Are you aware when I say to you, 'Sit properly with a straight back'? I'll tell you something very interesting. Brahmin boys in India up to the age of seven can do what they like, play around. At the age of seven they go through a certain ceremony and during that ceremony they are taught to sit completely still, with closed eyes. After the ceremony you become a real Brahmin and all the rest of it. From that day on you must sit properly, meditate, you are drilled. I'm saying that to show you how habits are built in, conditioned, and most of us are that way. To break down that conditioning you have to be aware of what you're doing. That's all.

Questioner: Breaking down good habits as well as bad?

KRISHNAMURTI: Everything. Habit means conditioning, a mechanical repetition, which is obviously not being sensitive. Now are you aware of what you're doing? When I say to you, 'Please dress differently,' are you taking my statement to help you to be aware and therefore sensitive, or do you resist it? What do you do? To be sensitive implies learning. I say to you, 'Jimmy, don't dress that way.' Will you treat it as a help to be aware, or do you resist? Or do you feel you're being hurt, 'I'm as good as you are, it's only your opinion' – all the battle of words and nonsense?

Questioner: So where do we react wrongly?

KRISHNAMURTI: You have to take into consideration conformity, imitation, fear of being hurt, trying to find your own freedom apart from mine. Dominic said, 'I don't want you to tread on my toes, I don't want to tread on yours.' Are you aware of the implications of all that's going on? If you're not, you become a hypocrite. Do you know you're hurt and that you don't want to be hurt any more?

Questioner: If you are giving your full attention to the moment, you haven't got time to remember that you've been hurt.

KRISHNAMURTI: No, but most of us don't know how to give complete attention to the moment. All that we remember is that we've been hurt and don't want to be hurt again. Have you got such hurts in you? What are you going to do about them. See what happens when you've got these hurts, they respond much more quickly than your reason does. Those hurts spring forward much quicker than, 'Let's find out, let's learn.' So you have to tackle that first. What will you do with those hurts?

Questioner: But those hurts are past.

KRISHNAMURTI: Are they past and dead?

Questioner: That's what is reacting.

KRISHNAMURTI: Yes.

Questioner: It doesn't have to react.

KRISHNAMURTI: Of course it doesn't have to, but it does. If you understand the whole mechanism of hurt, you will never be hurt again. Do you know what the mechanism of being hurt means? Find out. We have all been hurt some way or another. First, why have we been hurt?

Questioner: Sometimes it's because of our pride, our illusions.

KRISHNAMURTI: Why are you proud? What are you

proud about? Did you write a book? Or can you play tennis better, run faster than somebody else? We make these statements and say, 'Yes, I'm proud.' What does it mean? Because you're so nice-looking, so bright? And somebody comes along who is still brighter than you and you're hurt – you're jealous, you're angry, you're bitter, which is part of being hurt. So what will you do with those hurts which you have accumulated, which say, 'I must not be hurt any more'? What are you going to do, knowing that the hurts are going to respond so quickly?

Questioner: I would say that hurts are really disillusionments and disillusionments are really learning, so they are not hurts.

KRISHNAMURTI: Yes, but that is just an explanation. The fact remains that you are hurt. I put my trust in you and suddenly I find my trust has been betrayed: I get hurt. What is behind this hurt?

Questioner: I am sensitive.

KRISHNAMURTI: Is that it? Can sensitivity ever get hurt?

Questioner: (1) Only the 'I' in the middle of it.

Questioner: (2) The difficulty is really openness.

KRISHNAMURTI: Exactly. And sensitivity is intelligence. So when you say, 'I am hurt', who is the 'I' that is asserting this all the time? Do you want to learn about that 'I'? Or do you say, 'What is there to learn about the "I"?' Do you see the difference?

Questioner: Can you go into it a bit more?

KRISHNAMURTI: I am hurt by various people for various reasons. So I build a wall of resistance and you come along and say, 'Learn about it', 'Look at it'. Am I looking at the 'me' that is being hurt, the memories, which means another 'I' that is looking at it, a superior 'I' which says, 'I must learn about the lower "I".' Do you see the falseness of this?

125

You have established the 'I' which has to be learnt about. But there is no such thing as 'I' – it's just a series of memories. Actually, there is no 'I' except your memories of being hurt. But you have said, 'That is the "I" about which I'm going to learn.' What is there to learn about the 'I'? – it's just a bundle of memories, there's nothing to learn about it.

Questioner: You mean there's no self-knowledge?

KRISHNAMURTI: There is plenty, that's what we're doing— look how far we have moved in self-knowledge.

Questioner: If we are talking and I see something clearly, at that moment it's all right. Then afterwards the thing that I've seen becomes knowledge and I think I'm still seeing clearly. And somebody comes along and says to me, 'You're not seeing clearly,' and I say, 'I am', because I remember having seen clearly. Perhaps the reason I want to see clearly in the first place is just to build up this pleasurable feeling.

KRISHNAMURTI: Obviously. You've been hurt and you don't want to be hurt any more, and so you resist. What will you do? – knowing that prevents affection, love, every form of co-operation, every form of communication, of relationship. What will you do with that thing?

Questioner: You have to find a way of living where you are not building an image of yourself all the time.

KRISHNAMURTI: First of all, you have built an image; the next step is to prevent adding to it. There are two problems, aren't there? You have to prevent adding to it, as well as to cure and destroy the disease that you have. How will you set about this? I've explained it – you are not relating to it, that's all.

Questioner: You have to be highly sensitive all the time.

KRISHNAMURTI: Which means what?

Questioner: See exactly what the influences are . . .

KRISHNAMURTI: No.

Questioner : Stop the hurt.

KRISHNAMURTI: No. Look, be aware of what you are doing, of what you are thinking, feeling. And if I tell you to dress differently, don't resist and fight me but use my words to help you to be aware. You have been hurt, you have built a wall of resistance and I say to you, 'Sarah, don't do that because you'll prevent every form of relationship, you'll be miserable all your life.' Do you receive what I say to you with understanding, because it will help you to break down the wall? Or do you say, 'No, who are you to tell me, it's my way of living'? Which will you do, knowing that hurts and any wall of resistance prevent all relationships? Are you aware of this actually happening now? What's going to happen if I come along and say, 'Sarah, you're not so nice-looking as I thought you were.' Are you resisting?

Questioner : No.

KRISHNAMURTI: What is taking place then?

Questioner : I am learning about it and not resisting.

KRISHNAMURTI: Then what will you do?

Questioner : I'll see if what you say is right.

KRISHNAMURTI: So what does that mean? You have no conclusion about yourself. Is that what is actually taking place?

Questioner : It is right now.

KRISHNAMURTI: Take your hurts and go into it. Do you know what it means not to have any image about yourself?

Questioner : We can imagine about it.

KRISHNAMURTI: I can imagine good food, but I want to taste it in full! First, we said, 'We are hurt'; so we see actually, intelligently, sensitively, that we have built a wall round ourselves. Therefore we are hypocritical in saying, 'We will co-operate, we will do this together.' That's one point. The second point is: how am I, how is this mind to prevent image-making? Because if I have any image it is going to be hurt.

Questioner: Don't we make images of others?

KRISHNAMURTI: *Any* image, whether you make it of yourself or another, is still an image. Do you see the two problems? I have memories of being hurt, which create a wall of resistance; and I see that prevents every form of relationship. The other is, can the mind not make any more images at all? What am I to do with the past hurts, with the past images? Come on, you're nearly asleep! How will you help me to get rid of my past hurts? I want your help, which means I want to establish a relationship in which this thing will be dissolved.

Questioner: (1) You'll help me to learn that I am hurt and to see when my hurt is reacting. Therefore I can't just have a superficial relationship with you.

Questioner: (2) Yes, but I want to show you that I'm hurt.

KRISHNAMURTI: I want to be free of the past hurts, because I see logically, with reason, with sanity, that if the mind keeps those hurts it has no contact with anything – I am afraid all the time. Now do I see that very clearly? Do you understand it, see it as clearly as you see this table or chair? – which means you are giving attention to what is being said and watching it in yourself. Are you doing it, or are you casually looking at it with your mind somewhere else? If you give your attention to the past hurts, they'll obviously fall away. The next thing is, how are you going to prevent further images being put together? Suppose I come along and say, 'How very intelligent you are!' or 'You are such an ass, you're half asleep.' What will you do? How will you prevent immediately making an image when I say that?

Questioner: You are creating an image of me by your saying that.

KRISHNAMURTI: Obviously I'm an ass myself when I tell you you're an ass! But I'm asking you how to prevent images being formed – whether they be pleasurable or painful.

Questioner: You have to be awake to the image-making process.

KRISHNAMURTI: Help me to find out how to do it! Suppose I say to you, 'What a nice person you are,' that immediately brings a reaction and an image, doesn't it? Now, how will you prevent that taking place?

Questioner: The image is there already, it's been made – can we not just see that we have made this image?

KRISHNAMURTI: No. There are two things involved. First the past and secondly the prevention of new images being made. Because otherwise I'm going to be hurt again and I don't want to be hurt because I want to live freely, I want to have no walls around me. So what am I to do?

Questioner: I want to find out why I am flattered or hurt by what you say.

KRISHNAMURTI: One is pleasure, the other is fear.

Questioner: But what is the basis of this?

KRISHNAMURTI: You depend on my statement, I don't know why, but you do. That's not the point. How do you prevent this image being formed? Do you want to know? What will you pay for it?

Questioner: My life.

KRISHNAMURTI: What is the price of that life? – do you know what it means, Sir? It means you really are serious not to form any image about anybody, whatever they say. Are you willing to do that? How would you do it? I'll tell you. Each give me ten dollars. *(Laughter.)*

Questioner: We haven't got it.

KRISHNAMURTI: Watch it carefully. I've said this is a very serious matter, far more important than taking a degree. You pay a great deal to get educated, but you neglect this. Without this, life has no meaning and you don't even pay a cent to find out. Which means, you don't even give that much energy to find out. Jimmy says, 'I'll give my life to find out,' which means he's willing to go to the very end of it to find out. I said, 'Look, Jimmy, you've been hurt, and that hurt reacts in many ways. The root of that hurt is in an image you had of yourself, and that image doesn't want to get hurt.' You saw the truth of that. You are willing to go into it and you saw the truth of that and you said, 'I understood, I know how to deal with it. Any time it arises I'm going to be aware, pay complete attention to every moment when anybody says, "Do this, don't do that"!' Now why don't you give the same attention when somebody says, 'You're an ass'? Then you won't form an image. Only when you are inattentive, the old habit asserts itself. That means the mind says, 'As long as there is any form of resistance, all relationship has no meaning.' I see that very clearly. Not verbally, but I touch it, feel it. And I say, resistance exists because I don't want to be hurt. And why am I hurt? Because I have an image about myself, and I see there is not only the image about myself but there is another image in me which says, 'I must get rid of this image.' So there is a battle between the two images in me – the 'higher' image and the 'lower' image. Both images are created by thought. So I see all of that very clearly – clearly in the sense as I see anything dangerous. Therefore, the clarity of perception is its own action. Then I've finished with it, the past never comes again.

Now with that same attention I'm going to see that when you flatter me, or insult me, there is no image, because I'm tremendously attentive. Will you do this? It doesn't matter what is said, I listen, I don't say, 'You are prejudiced' or

'You are not prejudiced.' I listen because the mind wants to find out if it is creating an image out of every word, out of every contact. I'm tremendously awake, therefore I find in myself a person who is inattentive, asleep, dull, who makes images and gets hurt – not an intelligent man. Have you understood it at least verbally? Now apply it. Then you are sensitive to every occasion, it brings its own right action. And if anybody says something to you, you are tremendously attentive, not to any prejudices, but you are attentive to your conditioning. Therefore you have established a relationship with him, which is entirely different from his relationship with you. Because if he is prejudiced, you are not; if he is unaware, you are aware. Therefore you will never create an image about him. You see the difference? Will you do this? You have no idea what vitality you'll have.

Questioner : I think we have to help each other to do it.

KRISHNAMURTI: That's it, that is co-operation. You are helping me and I am helping you. You are learning from me and I am learning from you not to create images.

10

What do you think about all day? Watching thoughts. Identifying. Habits of thought and behaviour. The beginning and ending of thought.

KRISHNAMURTI: We are all terribly solemn this morning, aren't we? What do you think about all day long and why do you think about these things? Are you aware of what you are thinking or does one thought precede another endlessly and one is not aware of it? If you are aware of your thoughts from what source do they arise?

Questioner: From past experiences.

KRISHNAMURTI: Are you quoting what I said? Be quite clear that you don't say anything that you don't know yourself, don't say it if you haven't thought it out and worked it out, otherwise you get verbal and theoretical, so be careful. First of all what do you think about all day long? Is it a secret to keep to yourself, or can you share it with another?

Questioner: (1) I think about lots of different things.

Questioner: (2) About people at Brockwood.

KRISHNAMURTI: What is the central core of your thinking? You know there is peripheral thinking which is not really important, but at the centre, what is the momentum, the movement of that thinking? What is that 'me' that is so concerned with itself? I think about myself, that is the core, the heart of my thinking. And on the periphery I think about various things, the people here, the trees, the bird flying – these things don't really very much matter unless there is a crisis on the periphery and it affects the 'me' and the 'me' reacts. Now what is that centre from which you think – which is the 'me'? And why is there this continual occupation about oneself? I am not saying it is right or wrong, or 'How terrible', 'How childish' or 'How good' – but we see that we are occupied with ourselves. Why?

Questioner: Because we think it is important.

KRISHNAMURTI: Why do you give it importance?

Questioner: When you are a child you have to.

KRISHNAMURTI: Why do you think about yourself so much? See what is involved in this. Thinking about oneself isn't just a very small affair, you think about yourself in relation to another with like and dislike; and you think about yourself, identifying yourself with another – right? I think about the person I have just left, or the person I think I like, or the person with whom I have quarrelled, or the person whom I love. I have identified myself with all those people, haven't I?

Questioner: What do you mean by 'identify'?

KRISHNAMURTI: I love you, I have identified myself with you. Or, I have hurt her and you identify yourself with her and get angry with me. See what has happened: I have said something to her which is harmful and unpleasant; you are her friend, you identify yourself with her and get angry with me. So that is part of the self-centred activity, isn't it? Are you sure?

Questioner: But isn't it the other person who is identifying with you?

KRISHNAMURTI: Is it or is it not? Let's enquire. I like you, I am very fond of you – what does that mean? I like your looks, you are a good companion and so on. It means what?

Questioner: It means you are a better companion than other people and so I like being with you.

133

KRISHNAMURTI: Go a little deeper. What does it mean?

Questioner: You keep that person to yourself and exclude others.

KRISHNAMURTI: That is part of it, but go on further.

Questioner: It is pleasing to be with that person.

KRISHNAMURTI: It is pleasing to be with that person and it is not pleasing with another person. So my relationship with you is based on my pleasure. If I don't like you I say, 'I'll be off!' My pleasure is my concern, as is my hurt, my anger. So self-concern isn't just thinking about myself and identifying with this or that possession, person, or book. Is that what you do all day? There is the peripheral occupation, and also I am comparing myself with you; that is going on all the time, but from a centre.

Questioner: You read about the refugees in India and you haven't a personal relationship with them but you do identify with them.

KRISHNAMURTI: Why do I identify myself with those people who have been killed and chased out of East Pakistan? I watched them the other day on television; this is happening everywhere, not only in Pakistan, it is appalling. Now you say you identify yourself with all those refugees – what do you feel?

Questioner: Sympathy.

KRISHNAMURTI: Go on, explore it, unravel it.

Questioner: (1) Anger against the people who caused this.

Questioner: (2) Frustration because you can't do anything about it.

KRISHNAMURTI: You get angry with the people who do these things, who kill the young men and chase out old women and children. Is that what you do? You identify with this and reject that. What is the structure, the analysis of this identification?

134

Questioner: It is dualistic.

KRISHNAMURTI: Move on . . .

Questioner: You don't feel secure.

KRISHNAMURTI: Through identification you feel that you could *do* something?

Questioner: Even by taking one side you feel that you have a certain chance to do something.

KRISHNAMURTI: I am anti-Catholic, I identify myself with a group who are anti-clerical. Identifying myself with those, I feel I can do something. But go further, it is still *me* doing something about it, it is still the occupation with myself. I have identified myself with what I consider greater: India, Communism, Catholicism and so on. My family, my God, my belief, my house, you have hurt *me* – you follow? What is the reason for this identification?

Questioner: I separate myself from the rest of the world and in identifying with something bigger, that something becomes my ally.

KRISHNAMURTI: Yes, but why do you do this? I identify myself with you because I like you. I don't identify myself with him because I don't like him. And I identify myself with my family, with my country, with my God, with my belief. Now why do I identify with anything at all – I don't say it is right or wrong – what is behind this identification?

Questioner: Inward confusion.

KRISHNAMURTI: Is it?

Questioner: You are afraid.

KRISHNAMURTI: Push further.

Questioner: The confusion is caused by the identification.

KRISHNAMURTI: Is it? I am questioning you and you must question me too. Don't accept what I am saying, enquire.

This whole process of identification, why does it happen? And if I don't identify myself with you, or with something, I feel frustrated. Are you sure?

Questioner: (1) I don't know.

Questioner: (2) You feel unfulfilled, empty.

KRISHNAMURTI: Go on. I feel sad, frustrated, not fulfilled, insufficient, empty. Now I want to know why I identify myself with a group, with a community, with feelings, ideas, ideals, heroes and all the rest of it – why?

Questioner: I think it is in order to have security.

KRISHNAMURTI: Yes. But what do you mean by that word 'security'?

Questioner: Alone I am weak.

KRISHNAMURTI: Is it because you cannot stand alone?

Questioner: It is because you are afraid to stand alone.

KRISHNAMURTI: You are frightened of being alone, so therefore you identify?

Questioner: Not always.

KRISHNAMURTI: But it is the core, the root of it. Why do I want to identify myself? Because then I feel safe. I have pleasant memories of people and places so I identify myself with that. I see in identification I am much more secure, right.

Questioner: I don't know if you want to talk about this particular aspect, but if I see the killing in Vietnam is wrong, and there is a group of anti-war demonstrators in Washington, then I go and join them.

KRISHNAMURTI: Now wait a minute. There is an anti-war group and I join them. I identify myself with them because in identifying with a group of people who are doing something about it, I am also doing something about it; by myself I cannot do anything. But belonging to a group of people who demonstrate, who write articles and say, 'It is terrible,' I am actively taking part in stopping the war. That is the identification. We are not seeking the results of that identification – whether it is good or bad. But why does the human mind want to identify itself with something?

Questioner: When is it action and when is it identification?

KRISHNAMURTI: I am coming to that. First, I want to be clear in myself and in talking it over find out why I should identify. And when necessary I will identify. That is, I must first understand what it means to co-operate. Then, when I am really deeply co-operating, then I will know when *not* to co-operate. Not the other way round. I don't know if you see this? If I know what is involved in co-operation, which is a tremendous thing – to work together, to live together, to do things together – when I understand that, then I will know when not to co-operate.

Now I want to know why I identify myself with *anything*. Not that I shouldn't identify if there is a necessity of identification in action, but before I find out how to act, or with whom I can co-operate, I want to find out why there is this urge to identify. To have security? – is that the reason? Because you are far from your country, from your family, you identify with this house, with a group, to be safe, protected. The identification takes place because you feel, 'Here I am secure.' So is the reason you identify because you are insecure? Is that it? Insecurity means fear, uncertainty, not to know what to think, to be confused. So you need protection – it is good to have protection. Is that the reason why you identify?

What is the next step? In myself I am uncertain, unclear, confused, frightened and insufficient, therefore I identify myself with a belief. Now what happens?

Questioner: I find I am still insecure.

KRISHNAMURTI: No. I have identified myself with certain ideologies. What happens then?

Questioner: You try to make that your security.

KRISHNAMURTI: I have given various reasons for this identification: because it is rational, it is workable, all the rest of it. Now what happens when I have identified myself with it?

Questioner: You have a conflict.

KRISHNAMURTI: Look what happens. I have identified myself with an ideology, with a group of people, or a person, it is part of me. I must protect that, mustn't I? Therefore if it is threatened I am lost, I am back again to my insecurity. So what takes place? I am angry with anybody who attacks or doubts it. Then what is the actual thing that takes place?

Questioner: Conflict.

KRISHNAMURTI: Look: I have identified myself with an ideology. I must protect it because it is my security and I resist anybody who threatens that, in the sense of having a contradictory ideology. So where I have identified myself with an ideology there must be resistance, I build a wall round what I have identified myself with. Where there is a wall, it must create division. Then there is conflict. I don't know if you see all this?

Now what is the next step? – go on.

Questioner: (1) What is the difference between identification and co-operation?

Questioner: (2) It seems there has to be more understanding of co-operation.

KRISHNAMURTI: You know what it means to co-operate, to work together? Can there be co-operation when there is identification? Do you know what we mean by identification? We have examined the anatomy of it. Co-operation means to work together. Can I work with you if I have identified myself with an ideology and you are identified with another ideology? Obviously not.

Questioner: But people have to work together.

KRISHNAMURTI: Is that co-operation?

Questioner: No.

KRISHNAMURTI: See what is involved. Because of our identification with an ideology we work together, you protect it and I protect it. It is our security, in the name of God, in the name of beauty, in the name of anything. We think that is co-operation. Now what takes place? Can there be co-operation when there is identification with a group?

Questioner: No, because there is division. I find myself in conflict with members of the group, because I keep identifying with them.

KRISHNAMURTI: Look what is happening. You and I have identified ourselves with that ideology. Our interpretation of that ideology may be . . .

Questioner: . . . different . . .

KRISHNAMURTI: Of course. If you vary in the interpretation of that ideology you are deviating, therefore we are in conflict. Therefore we must both of us agree about that ideology completely. Is that possible?

Questioner: That is exactly what happens with a school. Instead of an ideology, you identify with a school and each person has his own concept.

KRISHNAMURTI: Yes, quite right – why?

Questioner: I sense that sometimes there is conflict here for just the reason you were giving when talking about an ideology. If you and I identify with the school, we think we are co-operating, but there isn't that spirit.

KRISHNAMURTI: Therefore I am asking, can there be co-operation when there is identification.

Questioner: No.

KRISHNAMURTI: Do you know what you are saying? *(Laughter.)* That is how everything in this world is working. Is that the truth? – that where there is identification there can be no co-operation? It is a marvellous thing to discover the truth of this. Not your opinion, or my opinion, but the truth, the validity of it. Therefore we have to find out what we mean by co-operation. You see there can be no co-operation when there is identification with an idea, with a leader, with a group and so on. Then, what is co-operation in which there is no identification?

Questioner: Acting in response to the situation itself.

KRISHNAMURTI: I am not saying you are not right, but can we work together when you and I think differently? When you are concerned with yourself and I am concerned with myself? And one of the reasons is, that knowing we cannot co-operate when we are thinking of ourselves, we try to identify ourselves with an ideology, hoping thereby to bring about co-operation. But if you don't identify, what is co-operation?

Here we are at Brockwood, in a school. We see there cannot be co-operation when there is identification with the school, with an idea, with a programme, with a particular policy of this and that. And also we see that identification is the cause of all division. Then, what is co-operation? To work together: not 'about something'. Do you see the difference? So before you do something together, what is the spirit of co-operation? The feeling, the inwardness of it, what is that feeling?

Questioner: Understanding, being completely open to it.

KRISHNAMURTI: Go a little deeper. We said identification is not co-operation. Are you quite sure on that point? And are you quite clear that co-operation cannot exist when each of us is concerned with himself? But you *are* concerned with yourself, therefore you have no spirit of co-operation, you only co-operate when it pleases you. So what does it mean to co-operate? We are not playing parlour games. What does it mean to co-operate when there is no 'me'? – otherwise you can't co-operate. I may try to co-operate round an idea, but there is always the 'me' that is trying to identify itself with the thing that I am doing. So I must find out why it is that I am thinking about myself all day long: how *I* look, that somebody is better than *me*; why somebody has hurt *me*, or somebody has said, 'What a nice person you are.' Now why am I doing this all day long? And at night too, when I'm asleep this goes on. *I* am better than you, I know what *I* am talking about, it is *my* experience, you are stupid, I am clever. Why?

Questioner: It seems a lot of it becomes a habit.

KRISHNAMURTI: What is habit?

Questioner: Not being aware.

KRISHNAMURTI: No. What is habit? – not how is it formed.

Questioner: Repetition of a movement.

KRISHNAMURTI: Right. Why is there a repetition of this movement? Why is habit formed? You will see something extraordinary if you go slowly. We have all got short hair or long hair – why? Because others do it.

Questioner: Is that habit or imitation?

KRISHNAMURTI: See what takes place. First you imitate others, then you say short hair is square.

Questioner: Is a custom a habit too?

KRISHNAMURTI: Yes. I don't want to go too quickly into this. Isn't all thinking habit? You agree?

Questioner: Well, it is something you do over and over again.

KRISHNAMURTI: Go on, see what you can discover for yourself when we go into this whole question of habit.

Questioner: It is really a situation with an old reaction, isn't it?

KRISHNAMURTI: A new situation we meet with old responses. Is not identification a habit?

Questioner: Yes.

KRISHNAMURTI: Because you are insecure. So do you know the nature of this machinery that makes for habit? Are you aware that you are always operating by habit? To get up at six o'clock every day; to believe 'all this'; to smoke, not to smoke, to take drugs – you follow? Everything is reduced to habit -- it may be of a week, ten days, or fifty years, but the habit is formed. Why does the mind fall into this groove? Haven't you asked yourself why you have a habit? – habit being merely tradition. Have you watched your mind working in habit?

Questioner: (1) It is easier.

Questioner: (2) It takes really a lot of energy to live without habit.

KRISHNAMURTI: I am coming to that. Don't jump, move from step to step. I am asking myself: why does the mind always live in habit? I thought that yesterday, I still think that today and I will think the same about it tomorrow – with slight modifications perhaps. Now why does the mind do this?

Questioner: One is half asleep.

KRISHNAMURTI: We said laziness is part of it. What else? It feels easier with habits.

Questioner: One is afraid of the unknown.

KRISHNAMURTI: I want to go a little deeper than that.

Questioner: The mind is afraid that if it doesn't maintain thinking in the same way, it will itself be threatened.

KRISHNAMURTI: Which means what?

Questioner: It sees a certain kind of order in habit.

KRISHNAMURTI: Is habit order?

Questioner: You can form a certain structure with habit, but that is not necessarily order.

KRISHNAMURTI: Which means that the mind functions in habit for various reasons, like a machine. It is easier, it avoids loneliness, fear of the unknown, and it implies a certain order to say, 'I will follow that and nothing else.' Now why does the mind function in a groove, which is habit?

Questioner: Its nature is that.

KRISHNAMURTI: But if you say that, then you stop enquiring. We know the reasons why the mind functions in habit. Are you actually aware of it? The highly psychopathic person has got a habit which is completely different from others. A neurotic person has got certain habits. We condemn that habit but accept others. So why does the mind do this? I want to go into it deeper, I want to see why it does it and whether the mind can live without habit.

Questioner: Because it feels it is the personality.

KRISHNAMURTI: We said that: the personality, the ego, the 'me' which says, 'I am frightened, I want order', laziness, all that is 'me' – different facets of the 'me'. Can the mind live without habit? – except for the biological habits, the regular functioning of the body which has its own mechanism, its own intelligence, its own machinery. But why does the mind accept habit so quickly? The question, 'Can it live without habit?' is a tremendous question. To say that there is God, there is a Saviour, is a habit. And to say there is no Saviour but only the State, that is another habit. So the mind lives in habit. Does it feel more secure in habit?

Questioner: Yes.

KRISHNAMURTI: Go slowly, which means what? Functioning in the field of the known it feels safe. The known is habit – right?

Questioner: Even then, we still say we don't feel safe.

KRISHNAMURTI: Because the known may change or may be taken away or get something added to it. But the mind is always functioning in the field of the known because there it feels secure. So the known is the habit, the known is knowledge – that is, knowledge of science, of technology, and the knowledge of my own experiences. And in that there is mechanical habit – of course. Now I am asking: can the mind move from the known – not into the unknown, I don't know what that means – but be free and move away from the borders of the known?

Look. If I know everything about the internal combustion engine, I can continue experimenting in the same direction, but there is a limitation. I must find something new, there must be some other way to create energy.

Questioner: Would the mind say that, if it wanted the security of the known?

KRISHNAMURTI: I am not talking about security at the moment.

Questioner: Are you saying that there has to be a lack of continuity? In technology, in order for something new to happen, there has to be a break in continuity.

KRISHNAMURTI: That's right. That is what takes place. Otherwise man couldn't have invented the jet, he must have looked at the problem differently. Are you following all this? My mind always works in the field of the known, modified, which is habit. In relationship with human beings, in thought – which is the response of memory and always within the field of the known – I am identifying myself with the unknown through the known. So I am asking: the mind must function with the known, because otherwise one couldn't talk, but can it also function without any habit?

Questioner: Does the mind ask that question because acting out of habit is unsuccessful?

KRISHNAMURTI: I am not thinking of success.

Questioner: But what would make the mind ask this?

KRISHNAMURTI: My mind says, 'This isn't good enough, I want more.' It wants to find out more, it can't find it within the field of the known, it can only expand that field.

Questioner: But it has to realize the limitation.

KRISHNAMURTI: I realize it, and I say to myself: I can function within the field of the known, I can always expand it or contract it, horizontally, vertically, in any way, but it is always within the field of the known. My mind says: I understand that very well. And so, being curious, it says: can the mind live, can it function, without habit?

Questioner: Is that a different question?

KRISHNAMURTI: Now I am talking psychologically, inwardly. Apparently all life, all the mental activity in the psyche, is a continuity of habit.

Questioner: Is there really an impetus or something . . .

KRISHNAMURTI: I am creating an impetus. The mind is itself creating the impetus to find out – not because it wants to find something.

Questioner: This is a very touchy point. This seems to be the key to some difficulty. Why – if I may just ask the question – does the mind say: I see the need for living without psychological habit?

KRISHNAMURTI: I don't see the need, I am not positing anything. I am only saying I have seen the mind in operation in the field of the known – contracting, expanding horizontally or vertically, or reducing it to nothing, but always within that area. And my mind asks, is there a way of living – I don't know it, I don't even posit it – in which there is no habit at all?

So we come back: do you know what you are thinking about all day? You say, yes, I am thinking about myself, vaguely or concretely, or subtly, or in a most refined manner, but always round that. Can there be love when the mind is occupied with itself all the time? You say, 'No'. Why?

Questioner: Because if you are thinking about yourself all the time, you can't . . .

KRISHNAMURTI: Therefore you can never say, 'I love you', until you stop thinking about yourself. When a man feels ambitious, competitive, imitative, which is part of thinking about oneself, can there be love? So we have to find a way of living in which habit is not. But habit can be used, the known can be used – I won't call it habit – in a different way, depending on the circumstances, the situation and so on. So is love habit? Pleasure is habit, isn't it? – is love pleasure?

Questioner: What do you mean by love, Sir?

KRISHNAMURTI: I don't know. I will tell you what it is not, and when that is not in you, the other is. Listen to this: where the known is, love is not.

Questioner: So one has to find out first what habit is, and then about non-habit.

KRISHNAMURTI: We have found it, we have said: habit is

the continuation of action within the field of the known. The known is the tomorrow. Tomorrow is Sunday and I am going out for a drive – I know that, I have arranged it. Can I say, 'Tomorrow I will love'?

Questioner: (1) No.

Questioner: (2) I do.

KRISHNAMURTI: What do you mean? 'I will love you to-morrow'?

Questioner: We promise that.

KRISHNAMURTI: In a church, you mean? That means love is within the field of the known and therefore within time.

Questioner: But if you love once, can you suddenly stop loving?

KRISHNAMURTI: I loved you once, I am bored with you now!

Questioner: If you love someone today you can love him tomorrow.

KRISHNAMURTI: How do you know? I love you today, but you want to be sure that I'll love you tomorrow, therefore I say, 'I'll love you, darling, tomorrow.'

Questioner: That is something else.

KRISHNAMURTI: I am asking: has love a tomorrow? Habit has a tomorrow because it continues. Is love a conti-nuity? Is love identification? – I love my wife, my son, my God? Therefore you have to really understand – not just verbally – the whole process, the structure and the nature of the known, the whole field of it inwardly, how you function always within that field, thinking from that field. The to-morrow you can grasp because it is projected from the known. To really understand this you have to understand all that we have said; you have to know what you think and why, and you have to observe it.

Questioner: You can know what you think, but you don't always know why you think it.

KRISHNAMURTI: Oh yes, it is fairly simple. I want to know why I think, why thought comes in. Yesterday I went to the tailor and I forgot my watch there. Last night I looked for it and I thought about it and said, 'How lazy of me, how inconsiderate on my part to leave it there, giving trouble' – all that went through the mind.

Questioner: When you say it was inconsiderate of you, you were identifying yourself.

KRISHNAMURTI: No, I forgot the watch. Which means they have to take the trouble to look after it, someone might take it, they will be responsible, all that. And I thought about it, and I know why this whole momentum of thinking arose from that one incident. I watched the whole flow of thought; you can know the beginning and the ending of thought – you look so mystified! – I have thought about it and I can end it. I left the watch there and I thought it might get lost; I have had it for a long time, I have cared for it. I would give it away, but not lose it. And it is lost! – finished. I didn't think any more about it. Now, to watch every thought, to be aware of it! Any thought is significant if you penetrate it; you can see the origin of it and the ending of it – not go on and on.

Questioner: And you say, Sir, if you see why the thought originated you will be able to see the ending of it?

KRISHNAMURTI: No, look. Is there an individual thought separate from another thought? Are all thoughts separate or are they interrelated? What do you say?

Questioner: They are interrelated.

KRISHNAMURTI: Are you sure?

Questioner: Well, they all come from one another.

KRISHNAMURTI: If I understand their interrelationship, or if there is an understanding of the background from which all thought springs . . .

Questioner: That is the difficult point.

KRISHNAMURTI: To watch without any question of wanting an answer means infinite watchfulness – not impatience – but watch carefully, then everything comes out. If you and I quarrel, I don't want to carry it in my mind, in thought, I want to finish it. I'll come to you and say, 'I am sorry, I didn't mean it' – and it is finished. But do I do that? Have you learnt a lot this morning? Not 'learnt' but 'learning': what it means to learn.

11

Opposition and conformity. Can we educate ourselves to meet life fully? The limitations of personal like and dislike. To be watchful.

Questioner: We were talking about why one can't say that one loves someone.

KRISHNAMURTI: Can we approach it in a different way? Do you know what aggressiveness is? It means opposition, to go against. From that arises the question: how are you going to meet life when you have passed through here and are so-called educated? Do you want to be swallowed up by the society, the culture in which you live, or are you going to oppose it, revolt against it, which will be a reaction and not a total action? Are you going to step into the easy way of life, conform, imitate, adjust to the pattern, whatever that pattern be, whether it be the establishment or an establishment of a different kind, and so on? Or are you going to be a totally different human being, who is aware and knows he has to meet adversity and opposition, and that therefore there is no easy way of satisfaction? Because most of us want a life of ease, of comfort, without trouble, which is almost impossible; and if you do meet opposition will you run away from it? 'I don't like this place, these people, this job', so I move away, run away from it to do something else which will be satisfactory. Do you use others for your own satisfaction? And is love the use of others, either sexually, or as companionship, or for one's own satisfaction, not superficially but much more deeply?

How are you going to meet all this, which is what life is? The so-called educated people in the world, who have been to college, to university, have got a good job, fit into a place and stay there and advance there. They have their own troubles, their own adversities.

One may pass some exam and get a job, or one may have been educated technologically. But psychologically one doesn't know anything about oneself. One is unhappy, miserable because one can't get this or that, one quarrels with one's husband or wife – you know all that goes on. And they are all very educated people who read books, disregarding the whole field of life. And the non-educated people do the same. You are going to be educated – I don't know why, but you are going to be – and then what? Lead a comfortable life? Not that one is against comfort, but if one is seeking comfort in life it becomes rather shoddy, rather shallow, and you have to conform to a tremendous extent to the structure of the culture in which you live. And if you revolt against the culture and join a group, which has its own pattern, you have to fit into that too.

Seeing that most human beings throughout the world want to be safe, secure, comfortable, lead a life of indulgence, a life in which they do not have too much opposition – where they conform superficially, but revolt against conforming, become superficially respectable but are inwardly rebellious, have a job, get married, have children and responsibility – but the mind wanting something much more than that, they are discontented, running from one thing to another. Seeing all of it, not just one segment, one fraction of it, but the whole of the map – what are you all going to do? Or is it a question that you cannot possibly answer at your age? – you are too young perhaps, with your own occupations, the other can wait.

Questioner: One knows what one would like to do.

KRISHNAMURTI: Do you know what you want to do?

Questioner: I know what I'd like to do.

KRISHNAMURTI: What would you like to do – like? I'd like to be the Queen of England! Or the greatest something or other and I can't. I haven't got the capacity. So when you say you'd like to do something that gives you pleasure, that gives you satisfaction, that is what everybody wants: comfort, pleasure, satisfaction. 'This is what I want to do because I feel happy in doing it.' And when you meet opposition along that path, you don't know how to meet it and then you try to escape from it. You know, this is really a very difficult question, it is not easy to say what one would like to do. This is a very complex question, that is why I said: is this asking too much? Or, at your age, are you already beginning to have the inkling of what you want to do, not only for the next year but for the rest of your life?

Questioner: We are not too young.

KRISHNAMURTI: I don't know. I don't know whether you are too old or too young. It is for you to answer, not for me. I am putting this to you, for you to find out.

Questioner: Some of us are already too old. We are already shaped. Already we have had experiences, etc., that makes us all very bored with life.

KRISHNAMURTI: You know, the other day we were talking about the fact that we are always thinking about ourselves. And when you are thinking about yourself, isn't it generally round what gives you the greatest pleasure? 'I want to do that, because it is going to give me tremendous satisfaction.' So how do you meet all these things? Shouldn't you be educated, not only in geography, history, mathematics and all the rest of it, but also in this field, where you have to discover for yourself how to live in this monstrous world – isn't that part of education? Now how could you set about educating yourself to meet this life? Do you expect somebody else to educate you, as they educate you in mathematics and other subjects?

Questioner: No.

KRISHNAMURTI: No? You are quite sure? If nobody is

going to educate you in the psychological, inward way of living, how are you going to do it? How are you going to educate yourself? You know what is happening in the world? Apart from the monstrosities and wars and butcheries and all the terrible things that are going on, people who think they know are trying to educate you – not in the technological world: that is clear, simple and factual.

The other day on television some bishop said: the knowledge of God is love and if you don't have knowledge of God you can't live, life becomes meaningless. You follow? Now there is that statement made most emphatically by a well-known bishop, or whatever he was, and I listened to it and I said: I am learning, I want to find out. I want to be educated. And he has reasonable explanations and you look at his collar, or his coat, or his beret, and you say, 'Oh, he is a priest, he is an old man, he is repeating old stuff' – that is nothing, and you push him away. And then a man comes along and offers you a pattern of living (listen to all this, please) which seems reasonable, logical and because of his personality, the way he looks, dresses, walks – you know all the tricks – you say, 'Yes, he has got something.' And you listen to him. And through the very act of listening you are being conditioned by what he says, aren't you?

Questioner: It depends how you listen.

KRISHNAMURTI: If you don't know how to listen to that bishop, you will say, 'How reasonable, he says we have lived this way for two thousand years, this is the right way, with the knowledge of God.' I listen to him and there is something that appeals to me and I accept it. I have been influenced by him. And I am also influenced by a man who says, 'Do this and you will have enlightenment.' So I am being influenced all round. What shall I do? I want to educate myself because I see very well nobody is going to educate me in that field. Because they have never educated themselves, they have never gone into themselves and examined, explored, searched out, looked and watched, but they have always conformed to a pattern. And they are trying to teach me how to live within that pattern, whether it is the Zen pattern, or the Christian, or the communist pattern; they have not educated themselves in the sense we are talking about, though they may be clever in argument and in dialectics. So as nobody is going to help me to educate myself inwardly, how shall I begin? And I see, if I don't do that I become a lopsided human being. I may be very good at writing an essay and getting a degree – then what? And the whole of the rest of my life is neglected. So how shall I educate myself, become mature in a field where very few people have taken the trouble to investigate, to enquire? Or they have done it and imposed their thinking on others, not helped them to find out for themselves. I don't know if you see that. Do you understand what I am talking about? Freud, Jung, Adler and other analysts, who have gone into this and stated some facts, traced all behaviour to childhood conditioning and so on – they have laid down a certain pattern and you can investigate in that direction and get more information, but it is not you learning about yourself. You are learning according to somebody else. So how will you set about it? – knowing what life is, what is happening in the world, wars, antagonism, politicians, priests, the hippies with their little bit of philosophy, the people who take drugs, the makers of communes and the hatred between various classes. Take all that outwardly; and inwardly people are ambitious, greedy, envious, brutal, violent, exploiting each other. These are facts, I am not exaggerating.

Now seeing all this, what shall I do? Shall I conform to some pattern which is comforting, which is what I want to do, a fulfilment for myself? Because if you don't have a certain spark, a flame in you now at the age of fifteen, sixteen, twenty or twenty-five, it is going to be very difficult when you are fifty. Then it is much more difficult to change. So, what shall I do? How shall I face all this, look at it, listen to all the terrible noise in the world ? – the priests, the technicians, the clever men, the workers, the strikes that are going on. Shall I choose a particular noise that appeals to me and follow that noise for the rest of my life? What shall I do? This is a tremendous problem, it is not a simple problem.

Questioner: I want to experiment.

KRISHNAMURTI: Experiment?

Questioner: Well, let things come to me.

KRISHNAMURTI: Listen to what I am saying. 'Seeing all this, I don't know what to do. Not knowing what to do, I am going to find an easy way out – I generally do.' Don't fool yourself. This is a tremendously complex problem.

Questioner: But to find the easy way out is still not real.

KRISHNAMURTI: Wait, I am not at all sure. I face it all, this tremendous roar that is going on, the shouting, the pushing, and I find there is an easy way out, I become a monk. That is what is happening in certain parts of the world, because people don't trust politicians, scientists, technicians, preachers any more. They say, 'I am going to withdraw from all this and become a solitary monk with a begging bowl' – they are doing it in India. Or not knowing what to do, you drift. Do you know what that word means? – to carry on from day to day, not to bother. Or if you must find a way out you force yourself, or you join a group that thinks it is tremendously advanced. Is that what you are all going to do? If I had a daughter or a son here, that would be my concern as a parent, I would feel tremendously concerned. And Brockwood is concerned – to me this is tremendously important. You can all go to colleges and universities and get a degree and a job. But that is too simple, it is a way out of it that doesn't solve anything either. So if I had a son or a daughter, I would ask, 'How are they going to be educated in the field where they themselves don't take an interest?' And the others don't know how to help them to understand that enormous field that has been neglected.

So I know what I would do in the sense that I would say to a daughter or son: Look, listen to all this, listen to all the noise that is going on in the world, don't take sides, don't jump to any conclusions but just listen. Don't say one noise is better than another noise; they are all noises, so just listen, first. And listen also to your own noise, your chattering, your wishes – 'I want to be this and I don't want to be that' – find out what it means to listen. Find out, don't be told. Discuss it with me and find out what it means first. Find out what it means to think, why you think, what is the background of your thinking. Watch yourself, don't become self-centred in that watching. Be tremendously concerned in watching, which is further enlargement of oneself.

Questioner: Did you say to be tremendously concerned with watching is further enlargement of the self?

KRISHNAMURTI: I said watch yourself. If I were a parent I would be tremendously concerned with the problem, the question how to educate people in this field where there is no real understanding or help. That is what I meant. But I said later on: if you watch yourself there is a danger of self-centredness – a tremendous danger. I must watch that too.

I also said I would discuss with the group, find out how you think, why you think and what you think. Not in order to change it, not to suppress it, not to overcome it, but to find out why you think at all. Go on, question it! I don't know if you have noticed that most books, all the social, religious, moral, ethical structure, the relationship between man and man and all the rest of it, are based on thinking.

Questioner: Yes.

KRISHNAMURTI: 'This is right, this is wrong, this should be, this must not be' – it is based on the structure of thought. Are you quite sure? – don't agree with me.

Now I want to find out if that is the way of living, to base everything on thought, on what I like and what I don't like, what I want to do, what I don't want to do. Probably you never think about it. Think about it now.

Questioner: Because your thinking is either you want to, or you don't want to. It all comes from the ' self '.

12

Learning about fear. Be awake to your conditioning. Dependence and standing alone. The state of creativity. To be sensitive. Awareness of beauty.

Questioner: Am I always self-centred, Sir? – it is a question that I find difficult to answer for myself.

KRISHNAMURTI: Here we are, in a beautiful countryside, living in a small community where relationship matters enormously. Can we live here with that quality of mind and feeling that is not wholly self-centred? Then, when we do leave this place – as we must – perhaps we shall be able to live in the world at a different level, with a different feeling and affection and with a different action. And to live like that, not just occasionally, but with a deeper sense of significance and worthwhileness and a feeling of sacredness, I think one has to be free of fear, or understand what fear is. Most of us are afraid of something, aren't we? Do you know what you are afraid of?

Questioner: Not at the moment.

KRISHNAMURTI: Agreed, because you are sitting here safely. But what is it that one is generally afraid of? Do you know what you are afraid of?

Questioner: The unknown.

KRISHNAMURTI: The unknown? What do you mean by the unknown? The tomorrow? What is going to happen to you, what the world will be like when you grow up and you have to face all the noise and the racket and absurdity of it? Is that what you are frightened of?

158

Questioner: Well, that is what I mean by the unknown.

KRISHNAMURTI: And how will you be free of that fear so that you can face it without darkness, without withdrawal, without a neurotic reaction to what the world is? How will you meet that? If you are afraid of it you can't meet it, can you? Discuss it with me! If you have any kind of belief as to how you should behave in the world, which is so chaotic, of which one is afraid, if you have already set a pattern of your behaviour with regard to that, won't that idea, won't that conclusion make it much more difficult?

Sophia, Laurence – do you know what you are afraid of? Are you afraid of your parents? Are you afraid of not being like the others? – having long hair, smoking, drinking, having a good time? Are you afraid of being rather odd, cranky, different? Are you afraid of being alone, standing alone? Are you afraid of what people might say? Of not making a good life in the sense of having money, property, house, husband or wife and all that – is that what you are afraid of? I feel if I don't smoke it is odd socially and I can't fit in; therefore I must force myself to smoke and do the things they do; I am a little frightened that I don't conform. Is that what you are afraid of: not conforming, not imitating, not fitting into the pattern, being square? So what are you afraid of? And throughout life are you going to carry any kind of fear with you?

Do you know what fear does? It makes you aggressive, violent. Or, you withdraw and become slightly neurotic, odd, peculiar; you live in a darkness of your own, resisting any kind of relationship with anybody, building a wall around yourself, with this nagging fear always going on. So if you don't solve these fears now, when you are young, fresh, have plenty of vitality and energy, later on you won't be able to, it will become much more difficult.

So shouldn't we consider what our fears are and see if we can't get rid of them now, while we are protected, while we

159

are here, where we feel at home, meeting each other all the time? Shall we go into this?

Questioner: Yes.

KRISHNAMURTI: How do you go into this problem of fear? For instance, you are afraid of the unknown, the unknown being the tomorrow, having to face the world which is so chaotic, mad, vulgar and violent. Not being able to meet it you are frightened of the future. How do you know what the future will be? And why are you afraid of it?

Questioner: Aren't we projecting an image of ourselves into the future? And then we are afraid of not being able to live up to that image.

KRISHNAMURTI: You have an image of yourself and if you don't live according to that image you are frightened. That is one of the fears, isn't it? He said just now he is afraid of the unknown – the unknown being the tomorrow, the world, his position in the world, of what is going to happen to him in the future, whether he will become a businessman or a gardener. How will you meet that? How will you understand the fear of the unknown? Because if you are going to be afraid now, as you grow older it will get worse and worse, won't it?

Why do you think about the future? Why do you look at the future in terms of what you are now? You are young, fifteen, seventeen, whatever it is, and how do you know what you will be in twenty years' time? Is there a fear because you have an image of yourself or of the world in twenty years' time?

Questioner: We have been conditioned to have such an image.

KRISHNAMURTI: Who conditions you? The society, the culture?

Questioner: The whole environment.

KRISHNAMURTI: Now why do you submit to it?

Questioner: It's fear again.

KRISHNAMURTI: That means what? Go into it. You feel
you have to conform and you don't want to conform. You
say, 'I don't want to conform', and yet you are conforming.
You have the image of yourself, which has been created by
the culture in which you live, and you say, 'That image
must conform to the pattern.' But it may not conform, and
you are frightened. Is that it? Why do you have an image
about yourself or the world? The world is cruel, brutal,
harsh, violent, full of competition and hate; everybody is
trying to get a job, struggle, struggle, struggle. That is a fact,
isn't it? Why do you have an image about it? Why don't
you say, 'That is a fact'? The sun is shining: that is a fact.
Or it is a cloudy day: that is a fact. You don't fight the fact.
That is what it is. Do you want to fit into that? Do you want
to accept the world as it is? Do you accept it and join it and
become like that, do you want to be that?

Questioner: Well, one doesn't.

KRISHNAMURTI: First see, just look. The world is like that,
isn't it? The world has created the culture in which you
were born. That culture has conditioned you and that conditioning says: you must conform, whether it is a Communist or Catholic or Hindu background. And now you are here
being educated, not merely with books but also deeply to
understand yourself. So you must ask yourself, do you want
to fit into all that? Do you want to conform to the pattern
to which culture has conditioned you, do you want to fit
into that?

Questioner: Obviously not.

KRISHNAMURTI: Don't say, 'Obviously not.'

Questioner: I think most people do.

KRISHNAMURTI: *You* – leave the others out.

Questioner: We don't.

KRISHNAMURTI: Don't say, 'Most people do'; they don't even think about it. They just run along with the rest. Here we are thinking about it, we are looking at it, we are questioning it. Do you know what it means not to conform to something? It means going against the whole structure of society. Morally, in business, in religion you are going against the whole culture; which means you have to stand alone. You may starve, you may have no money, you may have no job – you have to stand alone. Can you? Will you? You don't know, do you? – you may or may not.

That is one of our fears, isn't it? One of the great fears in our life is about conforming. If you conform, then you become like the rest – and that is much easier. But if you don't conform then the whole world is against you. And this is very serious, unless you have the intelligence to withstand the world; otherwise you will be destroyed. If you have fear you cannot have that intelligence. Or you will probably get married and your wife will want to conform and you won't. Then you are stuck! You have children before you know where you are and it's much worse – because then you have to earn money to support the children.

Questioner: Then you are back again.

KRISHNAMURTI: Then you are caught in a trap. So from now on you have to look at the whole problem, understand it, go into it. Don't just say, 'I am frightened.' You see the culture in which we are born makes us conform, doesn't it? It makes you conform and it makes you envious not to be like somebody else.

So conformity and comparison make you afraid – do you follow? At home, in school, in college, and when you are out in the world, life is based on it. So if you are frightened, then you are caught for ever. But you can say, 'I am not going to be frightened, let's examine it, let's find out how to live in the world which demands acceptance, conformity and comparison.' How can you live in this world without being frightened, without conforming, without always comparing yourself with somebody? Then, if you know how to live that way, you will never be frightened. You understand?

Begin here, don't look at the time when you will be fifty years old. Begin here, now, when you are very young, to find out how to live a really intelligent life in which there is no imitation, conformity and comparison, which is without fear. Your brain-cells, while you are young, are much more active, much more pliable, more inquisitive. Later on, when you are older, you will get conditioned, you will have a family, a house: 'I can't think of anything except business, it is dangerous to think more.' Now, how will you live a life in which you don't compare and conform, because you are not afraid. Which means what? Fear is engendered, is bred, when you have an image about yourself; and you have that image to conform. You, that image, wants conformity. Now we have to examine very carefully what conformity is. What do you mean by conforming? You have long hair; are you doing it because other boys and girls and older people have long hair? All the pop singers have long hair – have you seen their faces? Do you want to be like that? Having long and sloppy hair – which you have – do you consider that conforming? Are you doing it because others are doing it?

Questioner: If you have short hair you are also conforming.

KRISHNAMURTI: Are you conforming? You have long hair; are you conforming, wearing sandals because others are doing it? – walking in Piccadilly or Fifth Avenue with naked feet. Do you also walk around with naked feet?

Questioner: Usually I think it is the conditioning in which you are living.

KRISHNAMURTI: Which means: are you reacting against the short hair? I will tell you why I have short hair. I have had hair down to my waist, much longer than any of you here. And when I first came to England and went to school they used to say, 'Get your hair cut!' Give your minds to find out why you wear long hair. Are you doing it because others are doing it, or do you like it?

Questioner: I like it.

KRISHNAMURTI: What does that mean? You like to wear it because you are going to save money at the barber's? *(Laughter.)* You have to keep it clean, well brushed, otherwise it looks ugly. Do you do it because you like it? That is a good reason, isn't it? That means you are not conforming, because tomorrow the fashion will be short hair – will you all wear short hair then? So are you doing it because you want to do it, irrespective of what others do?

Questioner: Isn't it the same with clothes?

KRISHNAMURTI: Do you put on these strange clothes because others do?

Questioner: Every boy is concerned about his appearance to a greater or lesser extent.

KRISHNAMURTI: Right. You think this makes a good appearance, it's nice looking when you wear sloppy clothes?

Questioner: You might feel that yourself.

KRISHNAMURTI: Do you do it because you like it, or because you want to conform?

Questioner: Not necessarily because you want to conform.

KRISHNAMURTI: Find out! Don't say, 'Not necessarily.'

Questioner: I think it is all a matter of like and dislike.

KRISHNAMURTI: I am asking. The pop singers wear purple trousers and yellow shirts – you have seen that. They say, 'I like these clothes, they flatter me' – is that why you are doing it? So hair, clothes, the way you think, the way you feel – is it because the rest are feeling that way? The rest are

Frenchmen, Germans, Jews, Hindus, Buddhists, Catholics – and you become one or the other because that is the easiest. Is that why you follow? Or do you say, 'No, that is all wrong, I won't be like that.'

So first find out why you have long hair and clothes like this, whether you are American, French or German, so that you begin to exercise your own mind. You see, while you are young, if you are not revolutionary then – I don't mean throwing bombs, which is not revolution at all – if you are not enquiring, questioning, doubting, looking at yourself, finding out what *you* think, investigating the whole field of yourself, later on it will be much more difficult.

Questioner: I think the main point in all this is fear. For example, say I have long hair; if I cut my hair it's because I know that everything will go smoothly and there will be no problems at all. I feel I do most things for security, for ease.

KRISHNAMURTI: I understand. So you are frightened – why?

Questioner: Frightened that I don't fit in with the pattern that is going on.

KRISHNAMURTI: Then what will you do? Live with that fear? Why should you fit into the pattern?

Questioner: If you want to stay here it is better to do so.

KRISHNAMURTI: You are saying, if you want to keep alive, you must fit into the pattern. And do you want to live that way – fighting, quarrelling, hating, envy, struggle, wars?

Questioner: No.

KRISHNAMURTI: As we said the other day, to be really educated means not to conform, not to imitate, not to do what millions and millions are doing. If you feel like doing that, do it. But be awake to what you are doing – quarrels, hatred, antagonism, division between people where there is really no relationship at all, wars – if you really like living

that way. Then you will invite all the mess round you, you
are part of that, then there is no problem. But if you say, 'I
don't want to live that way', then you have to find out how
to live differently. And that demands intelligence. Conformity doesn't demand intelligence, it demands cunning-
ness.

The world is this and you are here to be educated in every
department of life, both inwardly and outwardly. Which
means: inwardly don't have fears. Not to have fears means
you must find out how to live without fear, therefore you
have to investigate what fear is. Enquiring into what fear is,
your mind becomes intelligent; that intelligence will then
show you how to live in this world sanely.

Fear is one of the greatest problems in the world, probably the greatest problem. So you have to face this thing,
you have to completely understand it and be out of it.

You said, 'I am afraid of the unknown, the tomorrow, the
future'. Why do you think of tomorrow at all? Is that a
healthy sign? You are young, full of the strange beauty of
this countryside, curious about birds, about living – why are
you concerned about tomorrow? Because your mother, your
father, the neighbours are already asking what will happen
to you tomorrow? They are frightened people – why do you
fall into their trap? The world is becoming more and more
populated – do you know what that means? In India, I
believe, twelve or thirteen million new babies are born
every year. And in China many more. The world is getting
fuller and fuller of people, and they all want jobs, they all
want homes, children, position, prestige, power, money.
The more you look at it the more frightened you get and you
say, 'What is going to happen to me?' How do you know
now what you will do or be like in twenty years' time? You
see what you are doing? While you are young, live, enjoy,
don't think about the future. If you live now without fear,
then when you grow up you will be the same, you will live –
it doesn't matter what you do, whether you're a gardener,
a cook, whatever it is, it will be a happy thing for you. But

if you say, 'My God, how shall I fit into this world, how shall I manage when I am thirty', then you are destroying yourself.

You see, each generation more or less conforms to the past generation, therefore no generation is ever a new generation. What we are trying to do here is to create a new generation. It may be forty people – that is good enough – who won't be afraid, who won't conform, who will have the intelligence to find out what to do when they grow up; this intelligence will tell you what to do. But if you are frightened, from now on you will be caught.

Are you afraid of standing alone? Do you know what I mean by that? Are you, Rachael? Are you afraid of being alone? – not in the dark. Alone means not to have companions, not to be dependent on people, on their flattery, on their encouragement, on their saying, 'You are marvellous.' Are you dependent on anybody? Obviously we are dependent on the milkman, on food, on who cooks it – we are dependent in that way. But emotionally are we dependent on anybody? Find out! Look at it. Does love demand dependence? 'I love you' – does it mean I depend upon you? Or do you depend upon me emotionally? I may earn the money, that is a different kind of dependence. But psychologically, inwardly, in our feelings, when we say 'I love', does that mean I depend upon you, that without you I would be lost? Is love like and dislike? That is a form of dependency – do you understand that? Do you see the difference between like and love, between love and pleasure? To like is a form of pleasure, isn't it?

Questioner: If I say, 'I like you', it means I choose, but if I don't choose then it is all right.

KRISHNAMURTI: Look! I am saying: do you depend psychologically on anybody? If you do, in that there is fear, isn't there? Because if anything happens to you I am frightened. I become jealous if you look at somebody else. Which means I possess you – right? I depend on you, therefore I must be assured that I possess you in every way, otherwise I am lost. Therefore I am frightened, therefore I become more and more dependent and more and more jealous. So do you depend on anybody? And all this dependence is generally called love, isn't it?

Questioner: Dependence is a fear of being without.

KRISHNAMURTI: Find out, don't agree, find out if you are dependent. And then find out why you depend and see what are the implications of that dependence – fear, loneliness, lack of comfort. If you don't depend on people then you are not frightened, are you? Then you don't mind standing alone. You are standing alone not out of fear; the moment you are alone you are much more honest, much more sure, nobody can corrupt you, there is no question of being hurt. So find out if you are dependent on people. And not only on people, on drink, tobacco, chatter, talking endlessly about nothing.

Questioner: We do depend on our parents, don't we?

KRISHNAMURTI: We depend on our parents because they have brought us into the world, they feel responsible and we depend on them because they give us money to be educated. That is a different kind of dependence.

Questioner: That is a necessary dependence.

KRISHNAMURTI: It is necessary. I depend on the postman. When I get into the train I depend on the engine driver.

Questioner: Is one dependent if one thinks incessantly of one object or person?

KRISHNAMURTI: Yes, obviously.

Questioner: It seems to me that one of the main things is that society is dependent on its art, which becomes part of any form of self-expression and art becomes incredibly important.

KRISHNAMURTI: 'Self-expression' – what does that

mean? 'I must express myself', 'I must be myself'. Look at it carefully. 'I' must express myself. 'I' must be myself. 'I' must find my identity – myself. You know all the phrases. Now what does that mean: 'I must be myself'? Is the 'I' the fear, the 'I' that is envious, the 'I' that says, 'I am so frightened of the future, what is going to happen to me?' The 'I' that says, 'It is my house, my book, this is my husband, my boy-friend?' That is the 'I', isn't it? And that 'I' says, 'I must express myself' – how silly it sounds! No?

Questioner: Isn't expression creativity?

KRISHNAMURTI: Find out. Is expression creativity? Painting a picture, writing a poem, making a pot – is that creativity? I am not saying it is or it is not.

Questioner: It does bring into being something that was not there before.

KRISHNAMURTI: To make something that was not there before is to be creative, is that it?

Questioner: That is not what you mean.

KRISHNAMURTI: I don't know. People say expression is creativeness. Follow this step by step – self-expression is creative. The self: what is that self?

Questioner: That kind of creativity is limited.

KRISHNAMURTI: Look at those words, 'I express myself and therefore I am creative.' What does it mean?

Questioner: It may be a sort of therapy, to be able to do that.

KRISHNAMURTI: You are saying, by expressing yourself you will become healthy, you will become sane? Listen: 'Self-expression is creative.' Think of that.

Questioner: I suppose it is just identifying oneself.

KRISHNAMURTI: Just look. What is the 'I'? Go into it, don't accept these terms: 'I am expressing myself.' What does it mean? Who is the 'I'? My long hair, my short hair, my anger, my jealousy, my memories, my pleasures, my dislike, my sex, my little enjoyment – is that the 'me'? It is the 'me', isn't it?, that wants to express itself – which is my anger, my jealousy, my this and that, whatever it is. Is that creative? So what is creativeness? This is an immense question. Does the creative man, or the creative mind, ever think about expressing?

Questioner: No.

KRISHNAMURTI: Wait, this is a little difficult. Don't say yes or no. Whoever says, 'I am expressing myself' ought to be kicked in the pants!

Questioner: To express something does not mean to be creative . . .

KRISHNAMURTI: Therefore, what does creativeness mean? I exist and express myself – is that creativity? Or is creativity when the 'I' is not? When the 'I' says, 'I must express myself by kicking somebody', the 'I' expressing itself is violence. So is the state of creativity the absence of the 'I'? When there is the absence of the 'I', do you know that you are creative? That is all! Have you understood? When you are doing something with a motive behind it – of becoming popular, famous, having more money – that is not doing something which you really love to do. A musician who says, 'I love music', but who is watching how many titled people there are in the audience, how much money he is going to make, he is not creative, he is not a musician; he is using music in order to become famous, to have money. So there can be no creativity if there is a motive behind it. See this for yourself.

So when we use these words, 'I must express myself', 'I must be creative', 'I must identify myself', it has no meaning. When you really see this, live that way, understand it, your mind is already free of the 'me'.

Questioner: Is it valid to make things of beauty?

KRISHNAMURTI: Valid for whom?

Questioner : For yourself.

KRISHNAMURTI: What do you mean, 'yourself'? Do you remember, we talked about beauty the other day? Look at that tree and the shadow and the sunlight: that is beauty. How do you know what is beautiful? Because somebody told you? A famous artist has painted a picture, or a great poet has written about that light and the tree and the clouds and the shadows and the movement of the leaves. And you say, 'He is a great man, I like that, it is beautiful.' Is beauty something that comes to you through another? Is beauty something that you have been told about? What then is the sense of beauty? Not what *is* beautiful, but the *sense* of beauty? Does this beauty lie in the building, in the tree, in the face of a person, in music, in a poem, in things outside? Or do the things you see become much more intensified because you have this sense, this sense of beauty? You understand what I mean? – because you have the feeling of beauty. Therefore when you see something extraordinary like that, you delight in it because in yourself you have this sense. Now how do you arrive at this, or happen to have this sense? How do you come by it? Can you come by it by training, through an image, through any amount of reading, studying, collecting paintings and having a lovely house? How does this happen?

Do you remember what we said the other day? It happens when you are physically very sensitive, watching – sensitive, not only about yourself but sensitive to others, to everything – sensitive to how much you eat, the way you sit, the way you talk, the way you walk. I am going to come down to something very practical. I have seen a lot of you eating: you touch something, lick your fingers thoroughly and go back and pick up something else – do you think that is to be sensitive?

Questioner : It is then on your own plate.

KRISHNAMURTI: I didn't mean that. You can do whatever you like on your own plate. But you lick your finger and pick up a piece of bread.

Questioner: It is unhygienic.

KRISHNAMURTI: I don't want to lick your spittle! I have seen everybody do it. First of all it is not hygienic. I touch my mouth and then pick up a piece of bread or something else – you follow? I have contaminated it.

You are unaware of what you are doing, you do it automatically. Now to do something automatically is not to be sensitive – that is all. So when you become aware of it, of the implications, you won't do it. When you sit down to eat, some of you don't chew your food at all. You just swallow it, and food is meant to be chewed. When you become aware of everything, you become sensitive and to be sensitive is to have an awareness of beauty, to have the sense of beauty. And without the sense of inward beauty you may do the most marvellous things, but it won't contain the flame.

13

Can one live sanely in this insane world? Is education at Brockwood bringing about an intelligence that will function in this world? Can one learn to look objectively and see the whole? The demand for security.

KRISHNAMURTI: The other day we were talking about sanity and mediocrity, what those words mean. We were asking whether living in this place as a community we are mediocre. And we also asked whether we are sane totally, that is bodily, mentally, emotionally. Are we balanced and healthy? All that is implied in the words sane, whole. Are we educating each other to be mediocre, to be slightly insane, slightly off balance?

The world is quite insane, unhealthy, corrupt. Are we bringing about that same imbalance, insanity and corruption in our education here? This is a very serious question. Can we find out the truth of it? — not what we think we should be in terms of sanity, but actually discover for ourselves if we are educating each other to be really sane and not mediocre.

Questioner: Many of us will have a job to which we have to go every day, many people will get married and have children — those are things that are going to happen.

KRISHNAMURTI: What is your place in this world as a human being who is supposed to be educated, who has got to earn a livelihood, where you may, or may not marry, have the responsibility of children, a house and mortgage and may be trapped in that for the rest of your life?

Questioner: Perhaps we are hoping somebody will look after us.

KRISHNAMURTI: That means you must be capable of doing something. You can't just say, 'Please look after me' – nobody is going to do it. Don't be depressed by it. Just look at it, be familiar with it, know all the tricks people are playing on each other. The politicians will never bring the world together, on the contrary; there may be no actual war but there is an economic war going on. If you are a scientist you are a slave to the government. All governments are more or less corrupt, some more, some less, but all are corrupt. So look at all this without getting depressed and saying, 'What am I going to do, how am I going to face this, I haven't the capacity?' You will have the capacity; when you know how to look you will have tremendous capacity.

So what is your place in all this? If you see the whole, then you can ask that question, but if you merely say to yourself, 'What am I going to do?', without seeing the whole, then you are caught, then there is no answer to it.

Questioner: Surely the first thing is for us to discuss these things openly. But I think people are a little frightened to discuss freely. Perhaps the thing they really care about will be threatened.

KRISHNAMURTI: Are you frightened?

Questioner: If I say what I want is a fast car, then perhaps somebody will question that.

KRISHNAMURTI: It must be questioned. I get letters questioning me all the time; I have been challenged since my childhood.

Questioner: Sir, there is something which always bothers me when these things are discussed. It is said we live in a highly mechanized industrial society and if some of us can opt out of it, it is because there are other people who do go to the office and work and become mechanical.

KRISHNAMURTI: Of course.

Questioner: We couldn't opt out of it without those people fulfilling their mechanized, miserable existence.

KRISHNAMURTI: No. How to live in this world without belonging to it, that is the question. How to live in this insanity and yet be sane?

Questioner: Are you saying that the man who goes to the office and leads an apparently mechanical life could do all that and yet be a different sort of human being? In other words, it isn't necessarily the system . . .

KRISHNAMURTI: This system, whatever it is, is making the mind mechanical.

Questioner: But does it have to make the mind mechanical?

KRISHNAMURTI: It is happening.

Questioner: All young people are faced with growing up, they see they may have to take a job which entails that. Can there be another response to it?

KRISHNAMURTI: My question is: how to live in this insane world sanely. Though I may have to go to an office and earn a livelihood, there must be a different heart, a different mind. Is this different mind, this different heart happening here in this place? Or are we just treading the mill and getting thrown out into this monstrous world?

Questioner: (1) There is no need any more to have a nine-to-five, six day a week job because of automation. What is happening is that this age is now giving us the extra time to attend to our other side.

Questioner: (2) But we were saying we want leisure and we don't know how to use leisure.

Questioner: (3) There is nothing wrong, surely, in earning a livelihood?

KRISHNAMURTI: I never said it's wrong to earn a livelihood; one has to earn a livelihood. I earn my livelihood by talking to people in many places. I have been doing it for fifty years and I am doing what I love to do. What I am doing is really what I think is right, is true; it is the way of living for me – not imposed on me by somebody – and that is my way of earning a livelihood.

Questioner: I just want to say that you are able to do that because there are people who fly the aeroplanes.

KRISHNAMURTI: Of course, I know that: without them I couldn't travel. But if there were no aeroplanes I would remain in one place, in the village where I was born and I would still be doing the same thing there.

Questioner: Yes, but in this highly mechanized society, where profit is the motive, this is the way things are organized.

KRISHNAMURTI: No, other people do the dirty work and I do the clean work.

Questioner: So one tries to do the clean work?

KRISHNAMURTI: It comes to that.

Questioner: But apart from earning a living, we have to begin to realize that to live sanely and yet earn a living in this world, there has to be an inner revolution.

KRISHNAMURTI: I am putting the same question differently. How am I to live sanely in this world which is insane? It doesn't mean I am not going to earn a livelihood, that I am not going to marry, that I am not going to take responsibilities. To live in this insane world sanely, I must reject that world and a revolution in me must come about so that I become sane and operate sanely. That's my whole point.

Questioner: Because I've been brought up insanely I have to question everything.

KRISHNAMURTI: That's what education is. You have been sent here, or you came here, contaminated by an insane world. Don't fool yourself, you have been conditioned by that insane world, shaped by past generations – including your parents – and you come here and you have to uncondition yourself, you have to undergo a tremendous change. Does that change take place? Or are we just saying: 'Well, we are doing a bit of good work here and there, day after day,' and by the time you leave in two or four years' time, off you go with a little patchwork done?

Questioner: There seems to be a conflict between what we want to do, what we desire to do, and what is necessary.

KRISHNAMURTI: What is it you desire to do? I want to be an engineer, because I see it brings in a great deal of money, or this or that. Can I rely on that desire? Can I rely on my instincts which have been so twisted? Can I rely on my thoughts? What have I to rely on? So education is to create an intelligence which is not mere instinct or desire or some petty demand, but an intelligence that will function in this world.

Is our education at Brockwood helping you to be intelligent? I mean by that word: to be very sensitive, not to your own desires, to your own demands, but to be sensitive to the world, to what is going on in the world. Surely education is not merely to give you knowledge, but also to give you the capacity to look at the world objectively, to see what is happening – the wars, the destruction, the violence, the brutality. The function of education is to find out how to live differently, not merely to pass exams, to get a degree, become qualified in certain ways. It is to help you to face the world in a totally different, intelligent way, knowing you have to earn a livelihood, knowing all the responsibilities, the miseries of it all. My question is: is this being done here? Is the educator getting educated as well as the student?

Questioner: Your question is also my question, I ask whether this education is happening here.

KRISHNAMURTI: You are asking whether such education is taking place here at Brockwood to help you to become so intelligent, so aware that you can meet this insanity? If not, whose fault is it?

Questioner: What is the basis which makes this education possible?

KRISHNAMURTI: Look, why are you being educated?

Questioner: I really don't know.

KRISHNAMURTI: Therefore you have to find out what education means, mustn't you? What is education? Giving you information, knowledge about various subjects and so on, a good academic training? That has to be, hasn't it? Millions of people are being turned out by the universities and colleges.

Questioner: They give you the tools to live with.

KRISHNAMURTI: But what are the hands that are going to use them? They are the same hands that have produced this world, the wars and all the rest of it.

Questioner: Which means the tools are there but if there is no inner, psychological revolution you will use those tools in the same old way and keep the rottenness going. That's what my question is about.

KRISHNAMURTI: If this revolution does not take place here, then why doesn't it? And if it does, is it actually affecting the mind, or is it still an idea and not an actuality, like having to eat three meals a day. That is an actuality, somebody has to cook, that's not an idea.

So I am asking you, is this kind of education we are talking about taking place here? And if it is, let us find out how to vitalize it, give life to it. If it is not, let's find out why.

Questioner: It doesn't seem to be happening in the whole school.

KRISHNAMURTI: Why not? It may be happening with a few individuals here and there – why isn't it happening with all of us?

Questioner: I feel it's like a seed which wants to germinate but the top soil is too heavy.

KRISHNAMURTI: Have you seen grass growing through cement?

Questioner: (1) Well, this is a weak seed, you see. (Laughter.)

Questioner: (2) But do we realize that we are mediocre and do we want to get out of it? – that's the point.

KRISHNAMURTI: I am asking you: Are you mediocre? I am not using that word in any derogatory sense – I am using the word 'mediocre' as it is described in the dictionary. You are bound to be middle class if you merely pursue your own little activities instead of seeing the whole – the whole world and your particular little place in the whole, not the other way round. People don't see the whole, they are pursuing their little desires, their little pleasures, their little vanities and brutalities, but if they saw the whole and understood their place in it, their relationship to the whole would be totally different.

You, living at Brockwood as a student in a small community, in relationship with your teachers and your fellow students, do you see the whole of what is going on in the world? That is the first thing. To see it objectively, not emotionally, not with prejudice, not with a bias, but just look at it. The various governments will not solve this problem, no politician is interested in this. They want more or less to maintain the *status quo*, with a little alteration here and there. They don't want the unity of man, they want the unity of England. But even there the different political parties don't say, 'Let's all join together and find out what is best for man.'

Questioner: But you are not saying it's not possible?

KRISHNAMURTI: They are not doing it.

Questioner: Are we?

KRISHNAMURTI: We are observing, we are first looking at the world. And when you see the whole thing, what is your desire in relation to the whole? If you don't see the whole and merely pursue your particular instinct or tendency or desire, that is the essence of mediocrity, that's what is happening in the world.

You see, in the old days the really serious people said, 'We will have nothing to do with the world, we will become monks, we will become preachers, we will live without property, without marriage, without position in society. We are teachers, we will go round the villages and the country, people will feed us, we will teach them morality, we will teach them how to be good, not to hate each other.' That used to happen but we can't do that any more. In India one still can. You can go from the north to the south and from east to west, begging. Put on a certain robe and they will feed you and clothe you because that is part of the tradition of India. But even that is beginning to fade, for there are so many charlatans.

So we have to earn a livelihood, we have to live in this world a life that is intelligent, sane, not mechanical – that is the point. And education is to help us to be sane, non-mechanical and intelligent. I keep repeating this. Now how do we, you and I, discuss this thing and find out first what we actually are and see if that can be totally changed? So first look at yourself, don't avoid it, don't say, 'How terrible, how ugly.' Just observe whether you have got all the tendencies of the insanity which has produced this ugly world. And if you observe your own particular quirks, find out how to change. Let's talk about it, that is relationship, that is friendship, that is affection, that is love. Talk about it and say, 'Look, I am greedy, I feel terribly silly'. Can that be changed radically? That is part of our education.

Questioner: It's when I feel insecure that I become silly.

KRISHNAMURTI: Of course. But are you sure? Don't theorize about it. Are you seeking security? – in somebody, in a profession, in some quality, or in an idea?

Questioner: One needs security.

KRISHNAMURTI: You see how you defend it? First find out if you are seeking security; don't say one needs it. Then we will see whether it is needed or not, but first see if you are seeking security. Of course you are! Have you understood the meaning and the implications of that word 'depending'? – depending on money, depending on people, on ideas, all coming from outside. To depend on some belief, or on the image you have about yourself, that you are a great man, that you have this or that, you know all this nonsense that goes on. So you have to understand what the implications of that word are and whether you are caught in those things. If you see you depend on somebody for your security then you begin to question, then you begin to learn. You begin to learn what is implied in dependency, in attachment. In security, fear and pleasure are involved. When there is no security you feel lost, you feel lonely; and when you feel lonely you escape, through drink, women or whatever you do. You act neurotically because you haven't really solved this problem.

So find out, learn what the meaning, the significance and the implications of that word are in actuality, not in theory. Learn: that is part of our education. I depend on certain people. I depend on them for my security, for my safety, for my money, for my pleasure, etc. Therefore if they do something which upsets me I get frightened, irritated, angry, jealous, frustrated, and then I rush off and put my claws into somebody else. The same problem goes on all the time. So I say to myself, let me first understand what this means. I must have money, I must have food, clothes and shelter, those are normal things. But when money is involved the whole cycle begins. So I have to learn and know about the whole thing; not after I have committed myself, then it is too late. I commit myself by getting married to somebody and then I am caught, then I am dependent, then the battle begins, wanting to be free yet being caught by responsibility, by the mortgage.

Here is a problem: Tungki says, 'I must have security.' I

answered: before you say 'I must', find out what it means, learn about it.

Questioner: I must have food and clothes and a house.

KRISHNAMURTI: Yes, go on.

Questioner: To have that I need to earn enough money.

KRISHNAMURTI: So you do whatever you can. Then what happens?

Questioner: To earn this money I depend on someone . . .

KRISHNAMURTI: You depend on society, on your patron, on your employer. He chases you around, he is brutal, and you put up with it because you depend on him. That is what is happening right round the world. Please look at it first, as you look at a map. You say: I have to earn a livelihood. I know in earning a livelihood I am dependent on society as it exists. It demands so many hours a day for five or six days a week and if I don't earn a livelihood I have nothing. That's one thing. And I also depend inwardly on my wife or a priest or a counsellor – you understand?

Questioner: So knowing all that I won't marry. I see the dependency, all the trouble that will come.

KRISHNAMURTI: You are not learning. Don't say you won't marry, see what the problem is first. I need food, clothes and shelter, those are primary needs and for those I depend on society as it is, whether it is communist or capitalist. I know that and I am going to look in other directions; I need security emotionally, that means dependence on somebody, on my wife, friends, neighbours, it doesn't matter who it is. And when I depend on somebody, fear always exists. I am learning, I am not saying what to do yet. I depend on you, you are my brother, my wife, my husband, and the moment you go away I am lost, I am frightened – I do neurotic things. I see dependence on people leads to that.

Also I ask: do I depend on ideas? On a belief that there

is a God – or not – that we must have universal brother-hood, whatever it is; that is another dependence. And you come along and say, 'What rubbish this is, you are living in a world of illusion.' So I get shaken and I say, 'What am I to do?' Then instead of learning about it I join some other cult. Do you see all this? Do you discover that in yourself you are insufficient and therefore you are dependent? Then you seek sufficiency in yourself: 'I am all right, I have found God, what I believe is true, my experience is the real thing.' So you ask: what is there that is so completely secure that it is never disturbed?

Questioner: I don't see the dependency on the two things you were talking about . . .

KRISHNAMURTI: We're asking what the implications of wanting security mean. We're looking at the map of security. It shows that I depend on food, clothes and shelter by working in a society that is corrupt – and I see what depending on people does. I am not saying this should be or that should not be. The map says: look, this road leads to fear, pleasure, anger, fulfilment, frustration and neurosis. And it also says: look at the world of ideas, depending on ideas is the most flimsy form of security, they are only words which have become a reality as an image; you live on an image. And that map says: be self-sufficient. So I depend on myself, I must have confidence in myself. What is yourself? You are the result of all this. So the map has shown you all these things and you ask now, 'Where is there complete security – including a job and all the rest of it?' Where will you find it?

Questioner: You find it when you have no fears.

KRISHNAMURTI: You haven't understood what I am saying. Put a map of this in front of you. Look at it all: physical security, emotional security, intellectual security, and security in your own thoughts, in your own feelings, in your self-confidence. You say, how flimsy all this is. Looking at it all and seeing the flimsiness, the invalidity, the lack of reality behind it, where is security then? It is learning about this which brings intelligence. So in intelligence there is security. Have you understood it?

Questioner: Can one live without security?

KRISHNAMURTI: You haven't learned to look first. You have learned to look through your particular image; that image has given you the feeling of security. So first learn to look at the map, put aside the image of what you think is security – that you must have it – and just look. What are the implications of wanting security? When you find there is no security in anything that you have sought, that there is no security in death, no security in living, when you see all that, then the very seeing of the fact that there is no security in the things in which one had sought it, is intelligence. That intelligence gives you complete security.

So learning is the beginning of security. The act of learning is intelligence, and in learning there is tremendous security. Are you learning here?

Questioner: In the family they say one must manage to earn a living, have a certain amount of knowledge. There is this idea about security, this basic necessity.

KRISHNAMURTI: Yes, Tungki, that's quite right. Your family, the tradition says you must have physical security, you must have a job, you must have knowledge, a technique, you must specialize, you must be this, you must be that, in order to have that security.

Questioner: It's an idea.

KRISHNAMURTI: I need money, that's not an idea – everything else is an idea. The physical continuity in security is the real thing; everything else has no reality. And to see that is intelligence. In that intelligence there is the most complete security; I can live anywhere, in the communist world or in a capitalist world.

Do you remember we said the other day that meditation is to observe? That is the beginning of meditation. You cannot observe this map if you have the slightest distortion in your mind, if your mind is distorted by prejudice, by fear. To look at this map is to look without prejudice. So learn in meditation what it is to be free of prejudice; that is part of meditation, not just sitting cross-legged in some place. It makes you tremendously responsible, not only for yourself and your relationship but for everything else, the garden, the trees, the people around you – everything becomes tremendously important.

To be serious is also to have fun. You can't be serious without having fun. We talked the other day about yoga, didn't we? I showed you some breathing exercises. You must do it all with fun, enjoy things – you follow?

Questioner: There are certain things like learning. I don't think it's possible to discuss them with a sense of fun.

KRISHNAMURTI: Oh yes! It is. Look, Tungki, learning is fun. To see new things is great fun; it gives you tremendous energy if you make a great discovery for yourself – not if someone else discovers it and tells you about it, then it's second-hand. When you are learning it is fun to see something totally new, like discovering a new insect, a new species. To discover how my mind is working, to see all the nuances, the subtleties: to learn about it is fun.

14

Violence in the world. The understanding of disorder and the roots of violence. Real work is 'to understand whether you live in disorder'.

KRISHNAMURTI: I have just come back from India. I have noticed that things are getting very bad, the world is in a very peculiar, destructive state, it is degenerating, people don't want to work, there are strikes. Apparently the war is over in Vietnam, but there is really no peace there. The communist world is also very disturbed; there is corruption everywhere, corruption in the sense not only of passing money under the table, but also in the sense that everybody is thinking selfishly, fragmentarily and thinking in circles. Also our artists can't go any further, they have come to the end of things. They have tried every kind of expression and they too have come to a point when they can't go any further. And poverty, as in India, of which you know absolutely nothing, is spreading, especially where there are severe droughts. With poverty goes degradation, every kind of violence goes on. Terrible things are happening in South America, in Brazil, and so on. I do not know if you are aware of all this: probably you are studying current history, current events, and one wonders what is going to be the outcome of it all. You are going to face all this when you leave this place.

So what is the relationship between the community here and the vast community of the world? What is going to happen to you all? This isn't a rhetorical, or merely an intellectually stimulating question. When you leave this place, what will be your fate – if I can use that word – what is going to happen? Do you know how to work, both intellectually and physically, and therefore are able to stand on your own against this current that is carrying people away? – the current of commercialism and vast selfishness. Either you are going to be drawn into it unknowingly, or knowingly, and if you know how to work, how to study, how to use your mind, then you may fit into it. Are you going to be sucked into the current, or stand alone?

So when one comes to Brockwood and sees the beauty of the winter, the bare trees, the lovely lines of the branches, the peace and quiet, the beauty of the place, one is rather shocked by the contrast of it all. And one wonders whether Brockwood offers you the opportunity – or it may and you do not utilize it – to really use your brain, your highest capacities, intellectual, physical and psychological. One wants to cry about the things that are happening, and here is a group, a community of fairly serious, fairly thoughtful people, where ideas and freedom and so-called discipline go together. Or is freedom a word that is misused and means doing what one wants to do?

What is it we are doing here together? Brockwood is a community, a so-called educational centre. I wonder if the word 'education' is the right word at all. When one uses that word as it is generally understood, it means learning out of books, storing up information and using it either selfishly or for a particular cause or a particular sect, and making oneself important in that sect or organization. Generally that is what is happening. Are we using our minds to their highest capacity, or are we just slowing down? Come on; I want to find out what you say, what you think. I'm afraid one has to be terribly serious, although you can laugh and play and have a good time; at the core one has to be terribly serious in this world – you are up against it.

How will you respond later on? That depends on what you are doing now. Whether you have observed what is happening in the world, how it is fragmented, broken up, each one fighting the other commercially, intellectually and emotionally; the different types of war, economic, social, class warfare, and the ordinary war of butchery, and the worship of success. You must face this. Have you the capacity to see it and not enter into the game at all? I think Brockwood offers an opportunity for you to have this inward strength to stand against all this. Whether you use that opportunity is up to you, and of course up to the grown-up people too. That is why I feel it is very important to know what it means to work; physically with your hands, psychologically with your mind – to work hard. Are you doing that here? Or is it all rather slack? Or do you say, 'We are free to do what we want'?

Questioner: What work is there to do besides just seeing all the problems? I mean that is the work, isn't it?

KRISHNAMURTI: But how do you see the problems? Everybody who is at all alive, a little watchful, sees these problems.

Questioner: Well, you have to see how you react, or how you act.

KRISHNAMURTI: How do you react? Do you see all this as though it were 'out there', or do you see it in relationship?

Questioner: I see it as an expression. I see it like art. All the problems are expressions.

KRISHNAMURTI: Do you consider all that is part of you? Or don't you belong to it? Are you an outsider looking in? Or are you looking without being an outsider? You observe it all: the worship of success, the brutality, the intellectual worship of things, the storing of knowledge. Are you all that, or are you different from all that?

Questioner: I don't feel either way.

KRISHNAMURTI: All that is the result of our greed, our ambition, competitiveness, worship of success, asserting oneself, thoughtlessness – are you free of all that?

Questioner: Maybe we are not free of it, but we are not part of it right now.

KRISHNAMURTI: You may be free of it. But if you are not free of it, are you aware that you are part of it?

Questioner: Every day you might say, 'I am not a part of this smoking, this drinking' – but it can happen to you any day. Even when you are in your room and you are quiet inside, you still can be selfish . . .

KRISHNAMURTI: What I mean is: do you look at all this as something different from you, or are you part of it? There may be moments when you are not – you may not be when you are thinking quietly – but as long as one is selfish, ambitious, greedy, possessive, one is that.

Questioner: At Brockwood we may feel we are not part of it, or we somehow fool ourselves that we are not part of it.

KRISHNAMURTI: I don't know, I am asking you. You may be fooling yourself thinking, 'We are different, we are young, therefore it is not yet our job to be concerned with it.' If you don't lay the foundation now, when you are young, I don't see how you are going to lay it later. In about ten years' time you will all be married and have children.

Questioner: There is some tendency to discriminate between what is nasty and what is necessary. To get down to practical things we have to associate ourselves, or be involved with everything that is here. A simple example is work in the garden – it is nice to work out there when it is sunny and warm . . .

KRISHNAMURTI: Yes, but it is awful on a day like this. Look, what are you all going to do? What is your future? What do you want to do? Or haven't you thought about it? If you haven't thought about it, just leave it alone, may be you are too young to think about it. But if you do think about it, what is going to happen to you?

Questioner: I don't quite understand what you mean. Is it what you can do, or what you think you want to do?

KRISHNAMURTI: Both. Can you separate what you can do from what you want to do? What is it you want to do?

Questioner: I could tell you what I don't want to do. I don't want to be part of what I see.

KRISHNAMURTI: I may not want to be part of all this mess, but I have to do something. I can't just say, 'I don't want to be that' and stay in my room. I have to eat, I have to clothe myself, I have to have shelter.

Questioner: You can work. You can leave here and just get a job.

KRISHNAMURTI: What is it the mind wants to do in this world?

Questioner: You can get a job.

KRISHNAMURTI: A job isn't the point. You can get a job if you are lucky enough, or you can live on somebody else. I met a man who had hitch-hiked from New York and worked his way across the sea and hitch-hiked from Paris to Delhi. You understand what that means? He was a Brahmin and a strict vegetarian, therefore all through the voyage he lived on cucumbers, a few fruits, an occasional orange for the three weeks. He said, 'I want to go to India, and when I get there I am going to spend my life as a really religious man' – whatever that may mean. Now what is going to happen to you? – I am really interested.

Questioner: It seems as though the more I look at things the less I want to do.

KRISHNAMURTI: The less you want to do anything.

Questioner: In a sense, yes. Not anything to do with business, most things are involved in this.

KRISHNAMURTI: I know, but nonetheless what will you do? You can't just sit back and say, 'I won't do anything'. You have got to eat, you have got to dress yourself and have got to pay to sleep somewhere.

Conversations with Students and Staff at Brockwood Park

Questioner: There are so few things you can do.

KRISHNAMURTI: Are there so few things? Do you want to hitch-hike to India? No, don't do it! Are there so few things to do in life without getting involved in all this mess?

Questioner: I would rather look at everything you can do, but everything seems to be contaminated by this mess.

KRISHNAMURTI: So that means that everything you do will be contaminated – is that it?

Questioner: Well, you have to deal with it.

KRISHNAMURTI: So how will you deal with it? You have to pay taxes and so on. Will you join a monastery – many people are doing that – but will you like that kind of living? Or is that question rather irrelevant to people who are still very young? But you are old enough to know that unless you lay a foundation now, and see how you observe – not analytically – what your reactions are, and why those reactions exist, unless you do that, it will be very difficult to face this.

Questioner: I wonder whether one can survive when one is put in a place where everybody is fighting with another.

KRISHNAMURTI: Yes, put yourself in that position. Have you thought about violence? What is involved in violence, how does it arise, what is the structure of violence? There is physical violence and there is the violence of obedience – are you obeying and therefore being violent? Do you understand what I mean? When I obey you and suppress what I think, that suppression will burst out one day. So there is physical violence and violence brought about through obedience, the violence of competitiveness, of conformity. When I conform to a pattern I am violent – you see the connection? When I live a life of fragmentation – that is, when I think one thing and say another, do another – that is fragmentation and that also breeds violence. I may be

191

very quiet, gentle, do all the work I am asked to do, but I flare up: which indicates there has been suppression in me. So violence is not just physical violence, it is a very complex question. And if you haven't thought about it, when you are faced with violence you will react most unintelligently.

Questioner: Can one live in this world without any violence at all?

KRISHNAMURTI: Find out, *work*. Find out how to live a life in which there is no violence.

Questioner: A minute ago you spoke about suppression. Maybe here, if we discuss things, it can come out and not be suppressed. I don't know if that is a form of suppression.

KRISHNAMURTI: Let us take it one by one. You know what physical violence is, getting angry, hitting each other, or somebody is bullying you verbally. That is one kind of violence. Obedience is violence, isn't it? Or would you say that is not violence? I obey when I keep to the left side of the road – is that violence?

Questioner: No. That is intelligence, if you didn't you would get run over.

KRISHNAMURTI: Yes, which means what?

Questioner: It is a fact.

KRISHNAMURTI: So there are facts and what else? Go on.

Questioner: And things that we produce in our head that don't really exist.

KRISHNAMURTI: I obey the law which says keep to the right in Europe and to the left in England. Is that violence? Obviously not. If you obey somebody who you think is superior in knowledge, is that violence? I teach you mathematics and you will discuss it with me, but in that there is some sort of imitation, conformity and obedience, isn't there? Is that violence? Society says you must go and kill the Muslims or the Communists – is that violence?

Questioner: Yes.

KRISHNAMURTI: Why? There is not only physical violence involved in it, but also so-called love of country, nationalism, a division of yourself as an Englishman, a German, a Russian, or a Muslim – which is a form of violence. So how will you have the insight to see where obedience is not violence and where it is? Do you see the difference? I conform, I imitate when I drive on the left. I put on trousers in this country, but when I go to India I put on Indian dress – is that a kind of conformity? And inwardly I conform to being a Hindu, to my tradition, to my beliefs – isn't that violence? So where is the line between violence and seeing for oneself where freedom is order? All violence is disorder. Don't misunderstand what I am saying and afterwards say, 'I won't conform' and go and do something silly. The whole world is involved in violence, in disorder of different categories. In the business world there is tremendous disorder, although there are marvellous companies run most efficiently; but they fight each other – there is disorder.

So I see disorder, and that freedom from disorder is order – right? There has to be the intelligence or insight to see that *any* movement towards disorder is violence. If I put on trousers in this country, is that conformity? To me it is not. But it is conformity to say, 'I am a Hindu, it is my tradition, my belief, my custom.' So I won't conform, because conformity there leads to disorder. So I wipe out Hinduism from my blood. That is real freedom. What does it mean to obey? 'You should do this', 'Keep to the left', 'Go to church', or 'You are an Englishman'. When you are aware of the factors of disorder, then you are free because there is order in your life.

This is real education: to live a life of tremendous order in which obedience is understood, in which it is seen where conformity is necessary and where it is totally unnecessary, and to see when you are imitating.

Questioner: Would you say that when you are imitating inwardly then you have conflict? For instance, when you learn a language and you do it because you feel you have to do it.

KRISHNAMURTI: There is nothing you *have* to do. If you are forced by circumstances, that is violence. To belong to a sect, to a group, to a country, that is really violence because it separates people. I see this happening – am I doing this? To find out if I am doing it, that is real work, that is what I mean by work, not merely gardening, cooking and studying; that is part of it, but the real work is to see, to understand whether you live in disorder. You may have tremendous order outwardly, put on clean clothes, wash and be punctual at all meals, but the real order is inside. And because you are in order you will do things in an orderly way. If you say, 'I will garden', you will garden whether it is foul or fair weather. Oh, you don't work – I have done all these things!

Questioner: We learn it in doing it. We are not suggesting that we retire to our rooms and find out.

KRISHNAMURTI: Good God, no! You learn while you are doing. The doing is the learning.

Questioner: To find out whether we are co-operating or conforming: if we are co-operating, then it really doesn't lead to contradictions.

KRISHNAMURTI: Either you have to co-operate because you are compelled, or violent circumstances compel you. Or you want to co-operate, you love to co-operate, you want to do things together. That is order; I can't live by myself in my room.

Questioner: And there is no contradiction there at all?

KRISHNAMURTI: Obviously not. But if you compel me, or circumstances compel me, or I feel that if I don't do it I'll be looked down upon, that is violence. But not if I see we must work together, that life is working together, that I can't live by myself. After all, I find out whether I am violent in doing things with you – how I play, how I talk, how I listen to you. In relationship I find out. Otherwise I can't find out, I can't sit in my room and try to find out whether I am violent. I can imagine I'm not violent, but the real test, the real action comes in relationship, to see if I am like that. That's real work. And if you do that you have tremendous energy because your life is in order.

15

What is the function of a teacher? Three streams of work. The function of Brockwood.

Meeting With Staff Only

KRISHNAMURTI: I don't know if you were considering what we were talking about the other day: how knowledge conditions the mind and whether it is possible to teach facts, give information and so on – all of which is knowledge – without conditioning the mind. One has given such tremendous importance to knowledge. To some Indian minds knowledge is a way to God. In the East, I think, knowledge represents a way of life in which the very studying of the sacred books – the Talmud, the various Sutras and the Koran – memorizing and repeating the texts, brings you nearer to what they call God, or Allah, or Jehovah.

We are saying that conditioning takes place not only culturally, in the sense of religion, social morality and so on, but also through knowledge itself. Is it possible to teach students and ourselves to free the mind from knowledge and yet use knowledge without causing the mind to function mechanically? If I were a teacher here, I would be greatly concerned how to bring about this unconditioning in myself and in the student. We went into that: in the very act of teaching I learn about my own conditioning and see the conditioning of the child and learn how to uncondition the mind. Now, can we go into this question of whether knowledge conditions the mind, and if it does, how to prevent it; how not to shape the mind in the very act of teaching and giving information.

Questioner: Knowledge itself doesn't condition your mind. It's your attitude to knowledge which conditions it; just having the facts in your head doesn't condition your mind.

KRISHNAMURTI: Why should I carry the facts in my mind? They are in the encyclopaedia, in the books – why should I carry all this in my mind?

Questioner: A great deal of the function of the mind is on a level where knowledge as a tool is necessary.

KRISHNAMURTI: If I want to build a bridge I must have a certain knowledge and experience, I need technical information. I use that knowledge to build a bridge. I see the necessity of a certain knowledge being held in the mind, but how am I to prevent that knowledge being misused by the engineer who says, 'I am going to use this for self-advancement'? Is that the problem?

Questioner: (1) Yes, it's the misuse.

Questioner: (2) Isn't it also that the mind can't keep still? One goes for a walk and one is thinking about building the bridge, not looking at the trees.

KRISHNAMURTI: But if I have got to build a bridge I have to think a great deal about it.

Questioner: It would seem that the more knowledge and information I can comfortably carry in the mind the better off I am, because I don't have to look it up in a book. I can refer to it very easily.

KRISHNAMURTI: So what is the function of knowledge? Here you are, teaching mathematics, geography, biology and so on; what is the function of it in life?

Questioner: It is a tool which the individual may use in his action.

KRISHNAMURTI: Action in a particular direction.

Questioner: It's the background you draw from in your action, whether it's knowledge from experience or from a book.

197

KRISHNAMURTI: I was talking yesterday to some parents in London. Their son is nineteen. When he was eighteen he was going to university and suddenly he dropped it all, took to drugs and gave whatever money he had to a particular guru, and he is meditating for an hour a day. The parents are concerned, they ask, 'What is going to happen to him?'

What is going to happen to these boys and girls we have here after you have taught them, given them all the information about art, music, geometry, history and English, whatever it is? They have acquired all that marvellous technical knowledge and then what happens to them? Will it make them glorified clerks in a rotten society? What for? If a boy does not go to university and get a degree, he finds it very difficult to get a job unless he has got some particular quality. So what is it we are trying to do? We give them all that knowledge and then leave a vast field, the other part of life, completely disregarded. Do you know what I mean?

Questioner: (1) I don't know if it's disregarded completely. The students find out in the course of this what they enjoy doing, where they can put their energy. They are finding out gradually what they can spend their life doing.

Questioner: (2) They are also coming into contact with other values because we listen to your talks together and as far as we can, we bring those to bear on our relationship with the student.

Questioner: (3) But the student has to get a sense of purpose in life that goes beyond the intellectual accomplishments which will take care of his daily living. He has to see the whole picture of living: ' What am I living for?'

Questioner: (4) Can a young person answer that question?

Questioner: (5) We can begin to enquire . . .

Questioner: (6) There is a great deal of uncertainty in young people and in other people's minds too, about the area where knowledge is good and useful and where it is irrelevant, where it goes wrong. I think the confusion between these two is constantly coming up among young people, among people who listen to you and have read your books. In a way it is clear and yet there is confusion about where the frontier lies between the two.

KRISHNAMURTI: Can I put the question differently? What is the function of a teacher?

Questioner: To indicate a way of living.

KRISHNAMURTI: Apart from, 'The teacher is the taught' – what is the function of a teacher?

Questioner: Could it possibly be to inspire the student with the kind of energy which he can then continue on his own?

KRISHNAMURTI: Do you inspire your students? I dislike that word 'inspire'. I don't want to inspire somebody – who am I?

Questioner: You don't inspire them, you release them to their own energy. You remove the thing which is impeding them.

KRISHNAMURTI: Is that the function of a teacher? – to make them study, to inspire them, encourage them, or stimulate them to study when they are not interested? You say that we have to help them to find their purpose in life.

Questioner: To find out what life is about in the sense of where I, as an individual, fit into the whole of life.

KRISHNAMURTI: Look at what is happening in the world. Thousands of boys are leaving university, taking to drugs, having individual sex or group sex, they run away, join appalling communities, sects, shave their heads, dance in the streets, give all their money to some guru.

Questioner: It's happening because they haven't had the right education.

KRISHNAMURTI: Are we giving them the right education?

Questioner: If we are, they won't do these things.

KRISHNAMURTI: No, not that they won't do it. What are we trying to do as teachers? We give them vegetarian food, ask them to get up in time, to be clean, keep their hair tidy, try to tell them to adjust themselves. What is it we are basically attempting to do here?

Questioner: The primary thing is to be aware of our conditioning in our relationship with the child.

KRISHNAMURTI: No.

Questioner: As it is, we have to spend so much time in relationship with the children, pointing out all these things which they do daily, like running along the corridors. In that way you are almost bound to spoil your relationship with the child. You see, a child here hasn't got one mother, he's got twenty, thirty mothers – all take it in turn to point out to him what he is doing wrong. What I want to know is, what kind of education, what approach do we have to the child that would make him not want to run down the corridor any longer.

KRISHNAMURTI: No. I would like to look at it this way – I may be wrong. You know what's happening in the world; politically all governments are corrupt, really corrupt, not superficially but deeply. And there are all these gurus going round the world, collecting money and followers, distorting the minds of young people; there are the drugs of various kinds, there is the army, there is business. Seeing what is going on, not abstractly but actually, what are we trying to do with these children? Make them fit into that?

Questioner: Partly to make them see all that as well; it's partly reflected in our own environment.

KRISHNAMURTI: No. Do let's be a little more concrete, a little more direct about it. What are we trying to do?

Questioner: (1) I want to encourage them to look at life with a greater seriousness. They seem very casual and relaxed, particularly the young ones.

Questioner: (2) When education was most significant to me it was in moments when my mental horizon was suddenly expanded through the influence of a teacher or through some cultural impact. There was an expansion of a sense of values which put things into perspective.

Questioner: (3) The keynote is the sense of values in a world where anything goes.

Questioner: (4) Aren't we trying to find out how to live differently? Ways have started which are so ugly, the ways of doing whatever you want, which is so shallow and pointless. Maybe there is another way for the child in which there is infinite depth.

Questioner: (5) The personality of the person who brings something to the child has to be acceptable to him. The child feels we are rather ordinary – I don't see why he should listen to us. I feel we have to bring into being a new quality in ourselves, primarily.

Questioner: (6) Do we, Doris? Primarily for ourselves?

Questioner: (7) Yes. I think so.

KRISHNAMURTI: Surely not.

Questioner: (1) Not in a self-centred sense, but primarily to find out, certainly for ourselves, a better way of actually living together.

Questioner: (2) Well, if we find that out for ourselves, aren't we finding it out as a whole, not just for our own selves?

Questioner: (3) Nothing is for our own, of course; we are not subtly trying to glorify our individual selves, on the contrary. But I feel that the quality of the being of each one here needs to be immensely more vital.

KRISHNAMURTI: 'It should be' – now we are lost!

Questioner: But what are we to do?

KRISHNAMURTI: I want to tackle it. Here I am, a teacher – what am I trying to do?

Questioner: So many of the students are already aware of the happen-

ings in the world outside, I think that's why some of the older ones are questioning the corruption of the government.

KRISHNAMURTI: Yes, then what? When they are faced with all this, when they go out into the world, will they be absorbed by it? Or just say, 'Sorry, I won't have anything to do with that', and move away from it?

Questioner: They have to find out for themselves.

KRISHNAMURTI: How will they find out, what will give them the light, the insight to say, 'I won't'?

Questioner: (1) That is what we are attempting to do here, and that is what they are also challenging.

Questioner: (2) That is why some of them came here.

KRISHNAMURTI: Now let's be clear – is that what we are trying to do? Helping them to see 'what is', the corruption and all the rest of it, and not to enter into that trap at all?

Questioner: That is only one part of it.

KRISHNAMURTI: What is the other part? Giving them knowledge? Helping them to have courage to battle? I asked the principal of one of the schools in India. I said, 'You have been doing this for nearly forty years, you have spent your life in this, has it been worthwhile?' He answered, 'Yes.' So I asked, 'In all those forty years has there been a boy or girl who was outstanding, who did not enter into this terrible morass of iniquity?' He answered, 'I don't know, very few were.' So I said, 'You mean in all those forty years you spent here only one or two have kept out of it?'

Questioner: Where does the trouble lie? – with the teacher or the taught?

KRISHNAMURTI: Both. You haven't got the material. If you want to make a good suit you must have good material.

Questioner: (1) I'd say the material is pretty warped already.

Questioner: (2) It's no good at all if you don't take any material you can find anywhere; the whole thing goes by the board if you are only having the best. But pick the first child you can from the slums of London. If it can be done at all, it can be done with that child.

Questioner: (3) I wouldn't use that phrase – good material or bad material – I would just say they are all human beings.

Questioner: (4) Then it has the implication that society is human beings all of whose intention is to do the right thing, to act intuitively, to be sensitive, aware, to be conscious of their actions. If that is so, then it seems to me that it defeats the purpose of having such a school, if we just take the mass of humanity and say everyone's intention is to be awake and to be sensitive, that influence plays such a small part. I think there is certainly a difference. I think it is a question of who comes here, who is here – whether it be staff or student – and what is their intention in being here.

Questioner: (5) There are some who have shown a predisposition to live in a different way, they have shown interest. There is an intelligence already.

KRISHNAMURTI: Now what part does knowledge play in that?

Questioner: A flower, a dog, has no knowledge and therefore it lives the sort of life it does. You need knowledge; how you use that knowledge gives the measure of you.

KRISHNAMURTI: So you are saying, how a human being uses knowledge is the really important thing.

Questioner: No, that can't be it.

KRISHNAMURTI: Why not?

Questioner: (1) Knowledge doesn't play a part in actual being.

Questioner: (2) Living properly does not depend at all on any sort of knowledge.

Questioner: (3) But living itself depends on knowledge.

Questioner: (4) What kind of knowledge are we talking about?

KRISHNAMURTI: Let's talk about what kind of knowledge we mean.

Questioner: Knowledge which is academic knowledge, which is scientific knowledge; it is part of what we are. At this moment we are using it for insight, if you like.

KRISHNAMURTI: Let's call it academic knowledge; that's one thing. Knowledge of how to live using that knowledge is another thing. Or is knowledge the whole thing? And where does freedom, where does spontaneity come in this? There is academic knowledge; if I learn about myself and use that knowledge about myself there is no freedom in that. I don't know if I am conveying this?

Questioner: Are you saying that one needs academic knowledge to learn about oneself?

KRISHNAMURTI: No. Must I go to a university to learn about myself?

Questioner: But going to university doesn't prevent you knowing about yourself.

KRISHNAMURTI: So there is self-knowing and academic knowledge, which is always the past, adding to it, taking away from it, moulding it – all that. If I say 'I know myself,' it is the knowledge which I have acquired in observing myself. That doesn't give me freedom – I am still caught in knowledge of myself.

Questioner: The idea I have about myself.

KRISHNAMURTI: Yes, Sir.

Questioner: That is using the ways of scientific knowledge and applying it to self-knowledge; that is the problem.

KRISHNAMURTI: No. Suppose somebody has never been

to university, he can learn about himself in his relationship to everybody.

Questioner: But does he build on that, does he store that knowledge away?

KRISHNAMURTI: The moment he stores it, then that becomes an impediment, therefore he is never free. I wonder if I am making myself clear?

Questioner: Are you saying that in learning about yourself there are two things. One is picking up little facts about yourself and storing them up and saying, 'I do this and this.' The other is a perception of that total process to a profound depth in which you suddenly see the whole thing and have then finished with it.

KRISHNAMURTI: Which has nothing to do with the accumulation of knowledge about yourself.

Questioner: You mean you see to a degree that makes all the knowledge of the little pieces put together disappear, because you have seen them.

KRISHNAMURTI: You see the whole of yourself . . .

Questioner: . . . and you therefore have freedom.

KRISHNAMURTI: That's right. That is freedom. If I learn about myself and say, 'I mustn't do this, I must do that' – you know all the petty little things that go on – that knowledge is going to completely cripple me: I daren't do anything freely, spontaneously. Now I think we begin to see what the different kinds of knowledge are. So what is it we are trying to bring about in the student? We don't only teach book-knowledge, that is understood. Then what is the other? Are you trying to help the student to know himself little by little? – collect knowledge about himself through little actions? Or are we trying to help him to have an insight into the whole of it? I think this is important. How is he to have a total insight into himself so that everything falls

205

into place? – all the little things – how to behave, how to have good relationships, everything falls into place. Now, how am I to convey this and help him to it?

Questioner: If one is indicating an action, a process in the present tense, it seems that one must be in that process oneself; one must be actively exploring it in oneself, otherwise it becomes just another fact that is added to all the others.

KRISHNAMURTI: Just another series of ideas; I understand that. Listen: I am trying to teach mathematics and also I am telling the student to get up early, to go to bed at the right time, eat properly, wash, etc. And yet I want to help him to have an insight which will enable him to get up at the proper time and do all the other things easily. Now there are three things I'm involved in: academic learning, telling him what to do, and at the same time I say to him, 'Look, if you get the insight everything falls into place.' I have all the three streams harmoniously running together. Now how am I to convey this? How am I to help him?

Questioner: He has to see where they all fit.

KRISHNAMURTI: No, no. Again, you are fitting him into this. Then he will say, 'All right, I'll fit into this.'

Look at the problem first. Academic learning is one stream. The other is the details, such as, "Get up, don't do this, don't do that' – which you also have to do. And the third stream is to say, 'Look, to be so supremely intelligent means you'll instinctively do the right thing in behaviour.' Let all three streams run together harmoniously.

Questioner: It's very difficult to . . .

KRISHNAMURTI: No, don't say it's difficult, don't say anything, but first see the thing. If you say it is very difficult, it is finished.

Questioner: The third element is a concept.

KRISHNAMURTI: No, it is not a concept, it is not an idea –

concept means an idea, a conclusion. I see the three things: the insight or the intelligence, the detailed behaviour, and academic learning; and I feel they are not moving together, they are not forming one harmonious river. So I say to myself: what am I to do, how am I to teach these three things so that they make a whole? When you listen to this you conclude, you say, 'Yes, I accept that as an idea.' I say it is not an idea. Then it becomes difficult, then you say, 'I don't know what to do.' But if it is a reality, how am I to convey the reality of it to the student – not the idea. Personally I have never had a problem or a conflict about all this.

Now how am I as a teacher, living here in a rather intimate relationship with the students – intimate in the sense of daily contact – how am I to show this? I am asking you, how will you show this to the child? – but not as an idea. If it is an idea, then it means you must practise it, you must battle with it, all that nonsense begins.

Questioner: Well, if it's meaningful to me, then it is meaningful.

KRISHNAMURTI: Is it meaningful to you?

Questioner: It is very, very meaningful.

KRISHNAMURTI: In what way? When do you use the word 'meaningful'?

Questioner: I feel these three elements are extremely important.

KRISHNAMURTI: Sorry, I refuse to say it is important.

Questioner: It is.

KRISHNAMURTI: Now how do you convey it to the child?

Questioner: Surely the beauty of insight conveys itself – the sheer beauty of it.

KRISHNAMURTI: Sir, do you know what you are saying? I won't listen, I am looking at that bird and you say, 'See the beauty of this.' Let the seed be born in him. How are you going to plant that seed? You understand?

Questioner: Yes, I understand. But I also see that if you can only plant the seed, and if relationship is not a meeting of one balanced mind with another balanced mind, then nothing comes of it.

KRISHNAMURTI: I agree. Now how do you propose this to happen? Take a boy, you help him, you give him everything he wants in the sense of good environment and good food, you tell him what to do, teach him academically and all the rest of it; then something happens and everything goes totally wrong for the rest of the boy's life. He takes to drink, women or drugs, cheats, does the most appalling things possible – he is finished. I have seen this happen. If you plant a seed in the ground it may die, but the seed itself is the truth of the tree, of the plant. Now, can this be done with us, with the children, with you and me?

Questioner: (1) It is something that can be done; by definition it can't be measured.

Questioner: (2) A child comes here perhaps from a very disturbed background for a very short time; we can only offer what we have. If we are fairly balanced, if we are very serious about it, if there is a right relationship, he takes that away when he goes out into the world.

KRISHNAMURTI: You are saying, 'If we are serious, if we are balanced' – but are we?

Questioner: I think that is one of the basic things we are questioning.

KRISHNAMURTI: Am I, are you, are we basically serious and balanced? – serious enough to say, 'Look', and convey it verbally and non-verbally?

Questioner: Sir, that is what I meant by beauty – the non-verbal conveying.

KRISHNAMURTI: To convey non-verbally one must be astonishingly clear oneself, limpid, and have that real seriousness, all that we said just now. Am I, are you?

Questioner: Aren't we teaching and learning together? Aren't we giving attention to every detail that happens during the day? So all the time you take the instance that presents itself. Because you feel so strongly about this the force is there and so you are dealing with every moment of the day. And it's not a correction; that is insight, if you like. And it's also linked with knowledge.

KRISHNAMURTI: I understand that. But I am trying to find out how I am to convey this thing? – the three streams moving together.

Questioner: You deal with the fact. To take one example: someone asked, 'Can I put the tent up?' And I said, 'Don't put it near the road.' She said, 'Why not? I'm a free person' – in other words, 'You needn't tell me.' So I told the person why. You go into it so that she understands the situation, which is factual; it includes the academic side and the intonation of the voice comes in too.

KRISHNAMURTI: I know.

Questioner: So it's not dealing with separate things all the time.

KRISHNAMURTI: Will this be conveyed to the student?

Questioner: It does sometimes and it doesn't at other times. You have to work at it and go into it again.

KRISHNAMURTI: So you are saying, one has to be at it all the time.

Questioner: All the time. Not in the sense of: 'You haven't done that.' That's pigeon-holing and petty and gives a wrong feeling, not insight. It's as though you came into a room and said, 'You don't do it that way.'

KRISHNAMURTI: I see that. I'm not questioning it, I think it's all right – I don't mean that in a patronizing way.

Questioner: The other side of it is, that if we only stay at that level and that becomes the element in which we are working in relating to the other, if that is so, then again it comes back to ourselves and our relationship – a balanced relationship between balanced people, if it is

*possible. If not, it is always a corrective measure and never a pene-
trating gesture, a penetrating relationship.*

KRISHNAMURTI: Yes, Sir.

Questioner: (1) Isn't that very action on a penetrating, deep level?

*Questioner: (2) It depends whether it goes to that level and you can
feel it. Perhaps I am talking too much about a specific example,
because I know the situation and I know that child and I know my
own relationship with that child on that level. Perhaps I am questioning whether or not it ever has penetrated the surface. I don't always
feel that is true in relationship with a young child. Do we have the
right to select and say: it seems that there is a possibility of insight
in one child, or that in another child there isn't that possibility. Do
we reject the child, or do we say: this is what this child needs and
relate it to that?*

KRISHNAMURTI: Take each child separately.

Questioner: That's it.

KRISHNAMURTI: Sir, all you have said is right. Is there a
different approach to this? What I mean is very difficult to
put into words. Can this seed be born without your doing
anything about it? We are doing something about it: my
relationship with the child, how I behave, what I do, how I
am – sentimental or balanced – learning about my self and
then helping the child – all that. We know that as probably
the only way. I am asking if there is another way at all, in
which this thing takes place without us doing something
about it – yet it takes place.

Questioner: Surely it must, in any real relationship . . .

KRISHNAMURTI: You are bringing in relationship . . .

*Questioner: Is there a way for a person to have a deep understanding
of the significance of his life? Is it possible to see . . .*

KRISHNAMURTI: . . . the whole thing instantly.

Questioner: Of course there must be.

KRISHNAMURTI: How?

Questioner: Surely a relationship in any situation is only a secondary thing – the insight is by definition itself. So if we are talking about education being basically self-understanding and awareness, then a community, an environment, a relationship can indicate something; but the individual must see, that must be the spring, it comes from inside, not from outside.

KRISHNAMURTI: I understand all that. I am trying to find out something else. A student comes here, terribly conditioned, or the family is broken up – this and that. And as a teacher, I also come here conditioned. I am learning about myself, I am helping in our relationship, I am quiet and so on. I am unconditioning myself and him in our relationship. We know that, we have discussed it, we have seen it. Now I am asking myself: is there a way of doing something which will bring about the seed to be born naturally in the person?

Questioner: What you are trying to say is: is there a way when a person can't say it for you? – yet you show me the way. Do you mean that?

KRISHNAMURTI: Not quite. Sir, can we produce a miracle?

Questioner: That's the question.

KRISHNAMURTI: Wait – you understand, Sir?

Questioner: Do we want to produce a miracle? Or do we just . . .

KRISHNAMURTI: I think both are involved – a miracle is also necessary. Do you understand what I mean by miracle? I don't mean something like Lourdes.

Questioner: Are you saying: if the seed is there, just like the seed in the ground, and the conditions are right, then it will flower?

KRISHNAMURTI: I don't mean it that way. We know the child as well as the teacher comes here conditioned and has to learn to uncondition himself. This unconditioning means: the academic side, behaviour in detail as well as seeing the totality, all of that running together. This is what I am trying to convey to the student and in that I am learning how to live that way. That takes too long. So I say to myself, 'A miracle must happen to change it instantly.' Maybe both together are necessary – the miracle as well as the other. Can we produce both? I think we can. And that's why, as you said just now, if we are balanced, serious – which means not sentimental, not verbal, not ideational but factual – if we are dealing with it in that way, the miracle comes.

Questioner: That's half the miracle, isn't it?

KRISHNAMURTI: Yes, Sir. I think that is what is necessary here – a miracle in that sense. That can only happen if we are really tremendously serious and not anything but factual. Can we convey to the student the factual? – never the ideal, never the 'what should be' – the sentiment involved in what 'should' be. I think then the miracle comes about. If you tell me I am a fool and I see it as a fact – the miracle then takes place. We are all brought up on 'what should be,' on ideation, a sentimental way of living, and these boys and girls are also used to that; they face facts only for a little while and turn it into sentiment. Can we convey to them never to enter into that field at all?

Questioner: It means that as a community we must put all this aside altogether, because otherwise our relationship is one of constant interpretation of another's behaviour, rather than actual awareness and deep understanding.

KRISHNAMURTI: Yes, absolutely.

PART II: QUOTATIONS

It is not that there must be an end to seeking, but rather the beginning of learning. Learning is far more important than finding.

As long as education is concerned merely with the culture of the outer . . . the inner movement with its immense depth will inevitably be for the few and in that there lies great sorrow. Sorrow cannot be solved, cannot be understood when you are running with tremendous energy along the superficial. Unless you solve this with self-knowing you will have revolt after revolt, reforms which need further reformation, and the endless antagonism of man against man will go on.

The heart of the matter is education, it is the total understanding of man and not an emphasis on one fragment of his life . . . All the enthusiasts for outward change always brush aside the more fundamental issues.

PART TWO

Conversations with Parents and Teachers

I

IT IS ALWAYS exciting to go to a new country, especially
when you are very young. One feels that very much in this
country where there is great physical freedom, where everyone seems to have so much energy, where there is a restless,
changing activity that seems to have no end. From coast to
coast, except for one or two cities, the great towns are all
alike. But the country is vast and extraordinarily beautiful
with its great spaces, deserts and long, winding deep rivers.
You can find all climates here from the tropics to high,
snowy mountains.

Overlooking the blue Pacific, in a large room several of us
were talking about education. A tall man in a tweed jacket
said: 'My sons and daughters are in revolt. They seem to
regard their home as a passage to somewhere else. They
have a feeling that they cannot be told anything, that they
have all the answers. They dislike any form of authority or
what they think is authority. They are naturally against
war, not because they have thought a great deal about the
causes of war, but because they are against killing other
human beings; yet they would approve of war for certain
causes. They are strangely violent, not only with us, but
they are against the government, against this and that.
They say they are against conformity but from what I have
seen of them and the friends they bring home they are as
conforming in their way as we ever were. Their form of conformity is long hair, dirty, bare feet, general slackness and
promiscuity. They have their own language. My son has
taken drugs. He could have done very well at the university
but he has dropped out. Although he is sensitive, intelligent
and what one would call thoughtful, he is caught up in this
maelstrom of chaos. His whole generation is against the
established order, whether it is that of the university, the

government or the family. Some of them read books on mysticism or indulge in black magic and other strange occult subjects. Some of them are really very nice, gentle, quiet, but with a sense of agonizing despair.'

Another man spoke. 'It is all very well while they are young but what will happen when they are older? In a country like this they can earn a few dollars easily and live on them for a while but as they grow older they will find it isn't as simple as they thought it would be. In revolt against our affluent society they turn to what they call a simple life; they want to go back to a primitive life and become like savages with many wives and children, digging a little in the garden and so on. They form communes. Some of them are serious but then others drift in and upset all their plans. And so it goes on.'

The third man said: 'I don't know the cause of all this. As parents we are blamed for their upbringing, for their revolt, for their lack of respect. Of course we parents have our own difficulties. Our families are broken up, we quarrel, we are bored with what we are doing, we are deep-down hypocrites. We keep our religion for the week-ends and the rest of the week we are merely tamed savages. Our children see all this – at least mine do – and naturally they have scant respect for us. We voted for our leaders and they despise those leaders. We have been to colleges and universities, they see what we are like and naturally – I don't blame them – they don't want to be like us at all. My son called me a hypocrite to my face and as he was telling a fact, I couldn't do anything about it. This revolt is sweeping the world.'

And the fourth said: 'If you ask them what they want to do, except for those who are committed to a particular political action – and fortunately there aren't too many of those – they will tell you, "We don't know and we don't want to know. We know what we don't want and as we go along we will find out." Their argument is very simple: "You knew what you wanted to do – get more money and a better position and look where you have brought the world. We certainly don't want that." Some of them want an easy, comfortable life, drifting, yielding to every form of pleasure. Sex is nothing to them. I wonder why all this has come about so suddenly in the last few years. You have often been to this country: what do you think is the cause of all this?'

Isn't there a deeper cause, a deeper movement of which perhaps the younger generation is not aware? In a society or culture that is so rich physically, with an astonishing technology, a people with so much energy may be living a very superficial life. Their religious beliefs and their struggles are not conducive to looking deeply within themselves. The outward thrust of material well-being with all its competitiveness, its wars, seems to satisfy them. They don't seem to want to investigate much wider or deeper, though they want to conquer space. They are concerned with the outer explosion – more of this and more of that – and are committed to the enjoyment of pleasure. Their God is dead, if they ever had a God. Volumes have been written about them, they have been analysed and put into categories. They even have classes where they learn to be sensitive. The feeling for vocation has come to an end. Life has become standardized and meaningless, with overcrowded cities, endless motorways and all the rest of it. What have you to offer to the young? What have you to give them – your worries, your problems, your absurd achievements? Naturally any intelligent person must revolt against all this. But that very revolt has in it the seed of conformity: conforming within one's own group and opposing another group. The young start out by revolting against conformity and end up conforming in a most absurd way just as thoroughly. You have lived for pleasure and they want to live for their own kind of pleasure. You have helped to bring about war and naturally they are against war. Everything that you have done, built and produced is for material well-being which has its place, but when that becomes an end in itself, then chaos begins. One wonders if you really love your children? Not that others do in other parts of the world; that is not the point. You may care for them when they are very young, give them what they want, give them the best food, spoil them, treat them like toys and use them for your own fulfilment and enjoyment. In this there is never any restraint, never a feeling for an austerity that is not at all the harshness of the monk. You have an idea that they must move freely, must not be repressed, that they must not be told what to do; you follow what the specialists recommend and the psychiatrists say. You produce a generation without restraint and when they revolt you are horrified, or pleased, according to your conditioning. So you are responsible for all this.

Doesn't this indicate, if one may ask, that there is no real love? Love has become merely a form of pleasure, a spiritual or physical entertainment. In spite of all the care you gave them when they were small you allow them to be killed. In your heart you want them to conform, not to your pattern as parents, but to the structure of a social order that is in itself corrupt. You are horrified when they spit on all this but in a strange way you admire it. You think it shows great independence. After all, historically you left Europe to be independent and so the circle is everlastingly repeated.

They were quiet. And then the tall man said, 'What is the cause of all this? I understand very well what you say. It is clear and obvious when you look at it. But underneath what is the meaning of it?'

You have tried to give significance to a life that has very little meaning, that is very shallow and petty, and failing in this you try to expand it on the same level. This expansion can go on endlessly but it has no depth, no profundity. The horizontal movement will lead to all kinds of places that are exciting and entertaining, but life remains very shallow. You may try to give depth to it intellectually but it is still trivial. To a mind that is really enquiring, not merely verbally examining or intellectually putting together hypotheses, to the enquiring mind the horizontal movement has very little significance. It can offer nothing except the very obvious, and so the revolt again becomes trivial, because it is still moving in the same direction – outward, political, reformatory and so on. The only revolution is within oneself. It is not horizontal but vertical – down and up. The inward movement in oneself is never horizontal and because it is inward it has immeasurable depth. And when there is really this depth it is neither horizontal nor vertical.

This you don't offer. Your Gods, your preachers, your leaders are concerned with the superficial, with better arrangements, better systems and organizations which are necessary for efficiency; but that is not the total answer. You may have a marvellous bureaucracy but it inevitably becomes tyrannical. Tyranny brings order to the superficial. Your religion which is supposed to offer depth is the gift of the intellect, carefully planned, recognized and believed in, a thing of propaganda. But this has no inward beauty. As long as education is concerned merely with the culture of the outer, specializing, enforcing conformity, the inner movement with its immense depth will inevitably be for the few, and in that also there lies great sorrow. Sorrow cannot be solved, cannot be understood when you are running with tremendous energy along the superficial. Unless you solve this through self-knowing you will have revolt after revolt, reforms which need further reformation, and the endless antagonism of man against man will go on. Self-knowing is the beginning of wisdom and it does not lie in books, in churches or in the piling up of words.

2

You CANNOT GET the whole feeling of a country unless you have lived in it for some time. Yet the people who live there, who spend their days and years and die there, seldom, it seems, have a feeling for the whole of their own country. People in this vast country with so many languages, generally are very secular and provincial. The different class divisions which at one time bound them together through religion, chants and stories, are rapidly going; this unity, this feeling of sacredness of life, of things that are beyond thought is disappearing. When you came year after year and spent several months here, you would notice the general decline; you would see in every big town the enormous increase in population; and walking down any street you would see people sleeping on the pavement, the terrible poverty, the dirt. Around a corner you would see a temple or a mosque full of people and beyond the town the factories, the fields and the hills.

It is really a very beautiful country with its high snow-covered mountains, its vast blue valleys, the rivers, the deserts, the rich red soil of the earth, palm trees, forests and the disappearing wild animals. The people are concerned with politics – one group against another group – the encroaching poverty, the squalor, the filth, but very few talk about the beauty of the land. And it is very beautiful in its variety, in the innumerable colours, in the vast expanse of the sky. You can get the whole feeling of the country with its ancient traditions, the mosques and the temples, the bright sunlight, the parrots and the monkeys, the thousands of villagers struggling with poverty and starvation, with lack of water until the rains come.

When you go up into the hills the air is cool and fresh,

there is green grass. You seem to be in a different world and can see many hundred miles of snow-covered mountains. It is startlingly magnificent and as you come down a narrow path poverty is there and misery; in a little shed there is a monk talking to his disciples. There is a feeling of great aloofness from all this. You meet people with brains that have been cultivated through many generations in religious thought and who have a peculiar capacity – at least verbally – to grasp the otherness of life. They will discuss sharply with you, quoting, comparing, remembering what has been said in their sacred books. It is all on the tip of their tongue, words piled upon words and the rich waters of the river pass by. You get the whole feeling of this extraordinary beauty, the vast mountains, hills, forests and rivers of the immense population, the varieties of conflict, the intense sorrow and the music. They all love music. They will sit listening by the hour in the villages, in the towns, absorbed in it, keeping time with their hands, with their heads, with their bodies. And the music is lovely.

There is tremendous violence, increasing hate, and a crowd around the temple on the hill. Millions make a pilgrimage to the river, the most sacred of all rivers, and come away happy and weary. This is their form of enjoyment in the name of religion. There are sanyasis, monks, everywhere. Serious ones and those who have taken to the cloth as the easiest way of living. There is endless ugliness and there is the great beauty of a tree and of a face. A beggar is singing in the street, telling of ancient Gods, myths and the beauty of goodness. The workers on the buildings listen to it and give of their little to the man who sings. It is an incredible land with its incredible sorrow. You feel all this deep down in yourself with tears.

The politician with his ambitions, everlastingly talking about the people and their welfare, the various petty leaders with their flocks, the division of language, the intense arrogance, the selfishness, the pride of race and ancient forebears, it is all there; and the strangest thing is children laughing. They seem to be so utterly ignorant of all this. They are poor and their laughter is greater than that of the rich and stuffy. Everything you can think of is in this land – deception, hypocrisy, cleverness, technology, erudition. A little boy in rags is learning to play the flute and a single palm tree grows in the field.

In a valley that is far from towns and noise, where the hills are the oldest in the world, a parent had come to talk of his children. Probably he never looked at those hills; they seemed almost to be carefully carved by hand, huge boulders balancing on each other. The sky that morning was very blue and there were several monkeys running up and down in the tree outside the verandah. We were sitting on the floor on a red carpet and he said, 'I have several children and my troubles have begun. I don't know what to do with them. I have to marry off the girls and it is going to be very difficult to educate the boys, and' – he added as an after-thought – 'the girls. If I do not educate them they will live in poverty, without a future. My wife and I are very disturbed about all this. As you can see, Sir, I have been well educated; I have a university degree and a good job. Some of my children are very intelligent and bright. In a primitive society they would do very well, but today you need to be highly educated in some special field in order to live a fairly decent life. I think I love them and I want them to live a life that is happy and industrious. I don't know what that word love means but I have a feeling for them. I want them to be cared for, well educated, but I know that once they go to school the other children and the teachers will destroy them. The teacher is not interested in teaching them. He has his worries, his ambitions, his family quarrels and miseries. He will repeat something he has learned from a book and the children will become as dull as he is. There is this battle between the teacher and the student, resistance on the part of the children, punishment and reward and the fear of examinations. All this will inevitably cripple the minds of the children and yet they have to go through this mill to get a degree and a job. So what am I to do? I have often lain awake thinking of all this. I see year after year how children are destroyed. Haven't you noticed, Sir, that something happens to them after they reach the age of puberty? Their faces change; they seem to have lost something. I have often wondered why this coarseness, this narrowing of the mind should take place in the adolescent. Is it not part of education to keep alive this quality of gentleness? – I do not know how to put it. They all seem suddenly to become violent and aggressive, with a stupid feeling of independence. They are not really independent at all.'

'The teachers seem to disregard this totally. I see my eldest boy coming back from school, already changed, brutalized, the eye already hard. Again what am I to do? I think I love them, otherwise I wouldn't be talking this way about them. But I find I cannot do anything, the influence of the environment is too strong, the competition is growing, ruthlessness and efficiency have become the standards. So they will all become like the others; dull, the brightness gone from the eye and the happy smile never to appear again in the same way. So, as a parent among a million other parents, I have come to ask what I am to do. I see what effect society and culture have but I *must* send them to school. I can't educate them at home; I have not the time, nor has my wife and besides, they must have the companionship of other children. I talk to them at home but it is like a voice in the wilderness. You know, Sir, how terribly imitative we are and children are like that. They want to belong, they don't want to be left out and the political and religious leaders use this and exploit it. And in a month's time they are walking in parades, saluting the flag, demonstrating against this or that, throwing stones and shouting. They are gone, finished. When I see this in my children I am so depressed I often want to commit suicide. Can I do anything at all? They don't want my love. They want a circus, as I did when I was a boy, and the same pattern is repeated.'

225

We sat very silently. The mynah bird was singing and the ancient hills were full of the light of the sun.

We cannot go back to the ancient system of a teacher with a few students living with him, being instructed by him and watching the way he lives. That is gone. Now we have this mechanical technology giving to the mind the sharpness of metal. The world is becoming industrialized and bringing with it its problems. Education neglects the rest of man's existence. It is like having a right arm highly developed, strong, vital, while the rest of the body withers, is weak and feeble. As a parent you may be an exception, but most parents want the industrial, mechanical process developed at the expense of the total human being. The majority seem to win.

Could not the intelligent minority of parents get together and start a school in which the whole of man is considered and cared for, in which the educator is not merely the informant, a machine which imparts a particular knowledge, but is concerned with the well-being of the whole? This means that the educator needs education. It means creating a place where the educator is being educated, and the help of a few parents who are deeply interested. Or is yours only a temporary, despairing cry? We don't seem to be able to apply ourselves to seeing the truth of something and carrying it out. I think, Sir, that is where the trouble lies. You probably feel very strongly for your children and how they should be. But being aware of what is happening in the world doesn't seem radically to affect you; you drift with society. You merely indulge in complaint and that leads nowhere. You are responsible not only for your own children but for all children and you have to gather up your strength together with others to create the new schools. It is up to you and not up to society or governments, for you are part of this society. If you really loved your children you would actually and definitely apply yourself to bring about not only a different kind of education but also a totally different kind of society and culture.

3

In the early morning before the sun was up there was a haze over the river. You could dimly see the other bank. It was still rather dark and the trees were shadows against the light sky. The fishing boats were still there: they had been there all night with their little lanterns. Dark and almost motionless, they had been fishing all night and there was not a sound from them. Occasionally of an evening you would hear the fishermen singing but now in the early dawn they were very quiet, tired out and sleepy. The current was carrying them gently along and they would presently return with their catch to their little village on this side of the river further down. As you watched, the rising sun would light up a few clouds in the sky. They were golden and full of that strange beauty of a morning. The light was spreading, making everything visible; the sun lately rising over the trees caught the few parrots screeching their way to the fields that lay beyond the river. They flew noisily, swiftly – green and red beaked – and they would return in an hour or more to their little holes in the tamarind tree across the garden. As you watched they blended into the green leaves so that you could scarcely see them except for their bright red beaks.

The sun was making a golden path over the water and a train rattled by across the bridge with a hideous noise; but it was the water that held the beauty of the morning. There was a wide expanse between this and the other bank, probably over a mile. The other bank had been cultivated for the winter wheat and it was now fresh and green and shimmering in the light breeze of the morning. As you watched the golden path became silver, bright and clear, and you could watch this light on the river for a long time. It was this light that penetrated the trees, the fields and into the heart of any man who looked at it.

Now the day had begun with all its accustomed noises but it was still the river that was so splendid, so full, so widely sweeping. It was the most sacred river in the world, sacred for many thousands of years. People came from all parts of that country to bathe in it, to wash away their sins, to meditate upon its banks still in their damp clothes, eyes shut and motionless. Now in the winter the river was low, but still very deep in the centre where the current was fairly strong. With the monsoon and the coming of the rains it would rise thirty, forty, sixty feet, sweeping everything before it, washing away the human filth, bringing down with it dead animals and trees until again it would be fresh, lovely and wide.

That morning there was something about it that was new, and as you sat and looked at it, the newness was not in the trees or in the fields or in those still waters. It was somewhere else. You looked at it with a new mind, with a new heart, with eyes that had no memory of yesterday and the squalor of man's activities. It was a splendid morning, cool, fresh, and there was a song in the air. There were beggars passing by and women in their dirty, ragged clothes carrying fuel to the town a mile or two away. There was poverty everywhere and utter callousness. But the boys who were cycling, carrying milk, were singing, and the older men walked along quietly, relentlessly, broken, thin and hard of body. But still it was a beautiful, clear morning and the clarity was not disturbed by the train rattling over the bridge, by the sharp cry of the crows or by the call of a man on the other bank.

The room with its verandah overlooked the river thirty or more feet below. There was a group of parents sitting on the floor on a fairly clean rug. They were all well fed, dark, cleanly and they had an air of smug respectability. They had come as parents to talk over their relationship to their children and their children's education. In that part of the world tradition is still very strong. They were all supposed to be well educated, or rather they had taken some degrees in universities and they had, in their opinions, fairly good jobs. Respect was ingrained in them, not only for their superiors in their professions, but also for religious people. That is part of this hideous respectability. Respect invariably shows disrespect, utter disregard for those who are below them.

One of them said, 'As a parent I would like to talk about my children, their education and what they are going to do. I feel responsible for my children. With my wife I have brought them up carefully, as carefully as we know how, telling them what to do and what not to do, guiding them, shaping them, helping them. I have sent them here to this school and I am concerned with what is going to happen to them. I have two daughters and two sons. As parents, my wife and I have done our very best and the best may not be sufficient. You know, Sir, there is an explosion of population, jobs are becoming more difficult, educational standards are lower and the students in the university are on strike because they don't want higher standards of examinations. They want easy marks; in fact they don't want to work or study. So I am disturbed and wonder how I, or the school or university, can prepare my children for the future.'

Another added. 'That is exactly my problem too. I have three children; the two boys are in the school here. They will undoubtedly pass some kind of examination, enter the university, and the degrees they will get are in no way near the European or American standards. But they are bright children and I feel that the education they are going to get, not in this school but later on, is going to destroy their bright eyes and the quickness of heart. Yet they must have a degree to find some sort of livelihood. I am greatly perturbed, watching conditions in this country, the over-population, the crushing poverty, the utter incapacity of politicians and the weight of tradition. I have to marry off my daughter; she will leave it entirely in my hands, for how can she know whom she should marry? I must choose a suitable husband who, with God's blessing, will have a degree and find a safe job somewhere. It is not easy and I am greatly perturbed.'

The other three parents agreed; they nodded their heads solemnly. Their bellies were full; they were Hindus to the core, steeped in their petty traditions and superficially worried about their children.

You have very carefully conditioned your children, though perhaps not deeply understanding the issue. Not only you but the society, the environment, the culture in which they have been brought up, both economic and social, have nurtured them, shaped them to a particular pattern. They are going to go through the mill of so-called education. If they are lucky they will get a job through your manipulations and settle down in their little homes with wives and husbands equally conditioned, to lead a monotonous, dull life. But after all that is what you want – a safe position, marriage so that they will not be promiscuous, with religion as an ornament. Most parents want this, don't they? – a safe place in society, a society they know in their hearts is corrupt. This is what you want and you have created schools and universities to bring this about. Give them a certain technological knowledge which will assure their livelihood and hope for the best, forgetting or purposely shutting your eyes to the rest of the human problem. You are concerned with one fragment and you will not consider the many fragments of human existence. You don't really want to be concerned, do you?

'We are not capable of it. We are not philosophers, we are not psychologists, we are not experts to examine the complexities of life. We are trained to be engineers, doctors, professional people and it takes all our time and energy to be up to date because so many new things are being discovered. From what you say, you want us to be proficient in the study of ourselves. We haven't the time, the inclination or the interest. I spend most of my time, as we all do here, in an office or building a bridge or attending to patients. We can only specialize in one field and shut our eyes to the rest. We haven't even the time to go to the temple: we leave that to our womenfolk. You want to bring about a revolution not only in religion but in education. We can't join you in this. I might like to but I just haven't the time.'

One wonders whether you really have not the time. You have divided life into specialties. You have divided politics from religion, religion from business, the businessman from the artist, the professional from the layman and so on. It is this division that is creating havoc, not only in religion but in education. Your only concern is to see that your children have a degree. Competition is growing stiffer; in this country the standards of education are being lowered and yet you keep insisting that you have no time to consider the whole of human existence. That is what almost everybody says in different words. And therefore you sustain a culture in which there will be increasing competition, greater differences between the specialists and more human conflict and sorrow. It is your sorrow, not someone else's sorrow. Yet you protest that you have no time and your children will repeat the same thing. In the West there is revolt among the students and young people; revolt is always against something but those who revolt are as conformist as those against whom they have revolted. You want your children to conform: the whole religious and economic structure is based upon this conformity. Your education sees to it that they do conform. Because you hope through conformity to have no problems you think that problems arise only when there is disturbance, change. You don't see that it isn't change that produces problems but conformity itself. You are afraid that any alteration in the pattern will bring about chaos, confusion, and therefore you condition your children to accept the traditional attitudes; you condition them to conform. The problems that arise from this conformity are innumerable. Every physical revolution starts out to break the physical pattern of conformity but soon establishes its own pattern of conformity, as in Russia and China. Each one thinks that through his conformity there will be security. With this movement of conformity comes authority. Education as it is now teaches the young to obey, accept and follow, and those who revolt against this have their own pattern of obedience, acceptance and subservience. With the increase of population and with the rapid growth of technology, you, the parents, are caught in a trap of mounting problems and the incapacity to solve them. This whole process you call education.

'What you say is perfectly true. You are stating a fact, but what are we to do? Put yourself in our place. We beget children, our appetites are very strong. Our minds have been conditioned by the culture in which we have been brought up, as a Hindu, or Muslim, and confronted with this enormous problem of living – and it is enormous – to live as you suggest as whole, complete human beings is bewildering. We are committed, we have to earn a livelihood, we have responsibilities. We cannot go back and begin again. Here we are caught in a trap, as you say.'

But you can see to it that your children are not caught in a trap. That is your responsibility: not to push them through some stupid examinations, but as parents to see that from their childhood they are not in any way caught in the trap that you and the past generations have created. Give of your time to see that you change the environment, the culture; see that there are the right kinds of schools and universities. Don't leave it to the Government. The Government is as thoughtless as you are, as indifferent, as callous. Instead of perpetuating the pattern of the trap, your responsibility now lies in seeing to it that there is no trap. All this means that you have to be awake, not only in your particular profession or career, but to the immense danger of perpetuating the trap.

'We see the danger but we seem to be incapable of acting even when we see it.'

You see the danger verbally and intellectually, and that seeing you call danger, which actually it is not. When you really see danger you act, you don't theorize about it. You don't oppose dialectically one opinion with another: you actually see the truth of the danger as you would see the danger of a cobra and you act. But you refuse to see this danger because it would mean you would have to wake up. There are disturbances and you are frightened of them. This is what prompts you to say that you have no time, which obviously is not so.

So as parents who are concerned, you must be committed utterly and completely to seeing that your children are not caught in the trap: therefore you will bring about different schools, different universities, different politics, different ways of living together, which means that you must care for your children. Caring for children implies the right kind of food, the right kind of clothing, the right kind of books, the right kind of amusement, the right kind of education; and therefore you are concerned with the right kind of educator. To you the educator is the least respected. Your respect is for those who have a great deal of money, position and prestige, and the educator who has the responsibility for the coming generation you totally disregard. The educator needs education as you, the parents, need education.

The sun was now beginning to get hot, there were deepening shadows and the morning was wearing itself out. The sky was less blue and the children were playing in the field, released from their classes, from the repetitive lessons and the drudgery of books.

4

IT WAS AN old, vast Byzantine building which had become
a mosque. It was immense. Inside they were chanting the
Koran and one sat beside a beggar on a carpet under the
huge dome. The chanting was magnificent, echoing in the
great space. There was no difference here between the
beggar and that well-dressed man, apparently well-to-do.
There were no women here. The men had their heads
bowed, muttering to themselves silently. Light came
through the coloured glass and made patterns on the carpet.
Outside were many beggars, so many people wanting
things; and down there was the blue sea, dividing the East
and the West.

It was a very ancient temple. They really couldn't tell
how old it was but they loved to exaggerate the antiquity of
their temples. One came to it through dusty, dirty roads
with palm trees and open gutters. They walked seven times
around the sanctuary and prostrated themselves as they
passed the door through which one saw the image. They
were devotees, completely absorbed in their prayers; and
here only the Brahmins were allowed. There were bats and
the smell of incense. The image was covered with jewels and
bright silk. Women stood there with hands raised and
children were playing in the courtyard, shouting, laughing,
running round the pillars. All the pillars were carved; there
was a great sense of space and heavy dignity, and because it
was so bright outside in the dazzling sun, here it was cool.
Some sanyasis sat meditating, undisturbed by the passers-
by. There was that peculiar quality of atmosphere that exists
when many thousands through the centuries come to pray,
worship and give offerings to the Gods. There was a tank of
water and they were bathing in it. It was a sacred tank be-

cause it was within the walls of the temple. It was very quiet in the sanctuary but the rest of the place was used not only for worship, for children to play in, but also by the older generation as a meeting place where they sat and talked and chattered about their life. Young students chanted in Sanskrit and later that evening about a hundred priests gathered outside the sanctuary to chant, praising the glory of the Lord. The chanting shook the walls and was a marvellous sound. Outside there was the hard blue sky of the south and in the evening light the palm trees were beautiful.

There was the vast piazza with a curving colonnade of pillars and the huge basilica with its tremendous dome. People were pouring into it, tourists from all over the world, looking with great wonder at the mass being performed; but there was very little atmosphere here – too many inquisitive people, hushed voices. It had become a show place. There was great beauty in the rituals, in the priests' robes but it was all man-made – the image, the Latin and the structure of the ceremony. It was made by the hand and by the mind, cunningly put together to convince one of the greatness and the power of God.

We had been walking through the English countryside among the open fields: there were pheasants, a clear blue sky and the light of the early evening. The slow quiet autumn was coming in. Leaves were turning yellow and red and dropping from the huge trees. Everything was waiting for winter, silent, apprehensive, withdrawn. How very different nature was in the springtime. Then everything was bursting with life – every blade of grass and the new leaf. Then there was the song of birds and murmuring of many leaves. But now though there was not a breath of air, though everything was still, it felt the approach of winter, rainy stormy days, snow and violent gales.

Walking along the fields and climbing over a stile you came to a grove of many trees and several redwoods. As you entered it you were suddenly aware of its absolute silence. There wasn't a leaf moving, it was as though a spell had been cast upon it. The grass was greener, brighter with the slanting sun upon it and you felt all of a sudden a great feeling of sacredness. You walked through it almost holding your breath, hesitating to step. There were great blooms of hydrangeas and rhododendrons which would flower in several months, but none of these things mattered, or rather they gave a benediction to this spot. You realized when you came out of the grove that your mind was completely empty without a single thought. There was only that and nothing else.

When one loses the deep intimate relationship with nature, then temples, mosques and churches become important.

The teacher said, 'How can one prevent, not only in the student but in ourselves, this competitive aggressive pursuit of one's own demand? I have taught now for many years in various schools and colleges, not only here but abroad, and I find throughout my teaching career this aggressive competitiveness. There is a reaction to this now. Young people want to live together in communes, feeling the warmth and comfort of companionship which they call love. They feel this way of living is much more real, full of meaning. But they also become exclusive. They gather together by the thousands for music festivals and in this living together they share not only the music but the enjoyment of it all. They seem so utterly promiscuous and to me it all seems childish and rather superficial. They may deny competitive aggression but it is still there in their blood. It shows itself in many ways of which they may not be aware. I have seen this same attitude among students. They are not learning for the sake of learning but for success, because of their desire to achieve. Some realize all this and reject it and drift. It is all right when they are young, under twenty, but soon they are caught and their drifting ways become the new routine.

'All this seems superficial and passing, but deep down man is against man. It shows in this terrible competition both in the communist world and in the so-called democracies. It is there. I find it in myself like a flame burning, driving me. I want to be better than somebody, not only for prestige and comfort, but for the feeling of superiority, the feeling of being. This feeling exists in the students though they may have a mild gentle face. They all want to be somebody. It shows in the class and every teacher is comparing A with B and urging B to be like A. In the family and in the school this goes on.'

When you compare B with A, openly, or secretly, you are destroying B. B is not important at all, for you have in your mind the image of A who is clever, bright, and you have given him a certain value. The essence of all this competitiveness is comparison: comparing one picture with another, one book with another, a person with another – the hero, the example, the principle, the ideal. This comparison is measurement between what is and what should be. You give marks to the student and so force him to compete with himself; and the final misery of all this comparison is the examinations. All your heroes, religious and worldly, exist because of this spirit of comparison. Every parent, the whole social structure in the worlds of religion, art, science and business is the same. This measurement between yourself and another, between those who know and the ignorant, has existed and continues in our daily life. Why do you compare? What is the need of measurement? Is it an escape from yourself, from your own shallowness, emptiness and insufficiency? This attachment to measurement of what you have been and what you will be divides life and thereby all conflict begins.

'But surely, Sir, you must compare. You compare when you choose this or that house, this or that cloth. Choice is necessary.'

We are not talking about such superficial choice. That is inevitable. But we are concerned with the psychological, the inward comparative spirit which brings about competitiveness with its aggression and ruthlessness. You are asking why, as a teacher and human being, you have this spirit, why you compete, why you compare. If you do not understand this in yourself, you will be encouraging competition, consciously or unconsciously, in the student. You will set up the image of the hero – political, economic or moral. The saint wants to break records as much as the man who plays cricket. Really there is not much difference between them, for both have this comparative evaluation of life. If you seriously ask yourself why you compare and whether it is possible to live a life without comparison, if you seriously enquire into this, not merely intellectually but actually, and go into yourself deeply putting away this competitive aggression, would you not find that there is a deep fear of being nothing? By putting on different masks, according to the culture and society you live in, you cover the fear of not being and not becoming: the becoming as something better than what is – something greater, nobler. When you observe what actually is, it is also the result of previous conditioning, of measurement. When you understand the real significance of measurement and comparison then there is freedom from what is.

After a moment the teacher said, 'If there is not the encouragement of comparison the student will not study. He needs to be encouraged, to be goaded, to be cajoled, and also he wants to know how he is doing. When he takes an examination he has the right to know how many of his answers were correct and how close his knowledge is to what was taught.'

If I may point out, Sirs, he is like you. He is conditioned by society and the culture in which he lives. One has to learn about this competitive aggression which comes through comparison and measurement. This may bring about an accumulation of great knowledge, you may achieve a great many things, but it denies love and it denies also the understanding of oneself. Understanding oneself is of far greater importance than becoming somebody. The very words we use are comparative – better, greater, nobler.

'But, Sir, I must ask – how does either student or teacher evaluate his factual knowledge of a subject without some kind of examination?'

Doesn't this imply that in everyday teaching and learning, through discussion, study, the teacher will become aware of how much factual knowledge the student has absorbed? This really means, doesn't it, that the teacher has to keep a close watch on the student, observe his capacity, what is going on in his head. That means you must care for the student.

'There is so much to convey to the student.'

What is it you want to convey to him? To live a non-competitive life? To explain to him the machinery of comparison and what it does? Tell him in words and convince him intellectually? You yourselves may see this intellectually or verbally understand it, but is it not possible to find a way of living in which all comparison ceases? You as teachers and human beings have to live that way. Only then can you convey it to the student and it will have truth behind it. But if you don't live that way you are only playing with words and hypocrisy follows. To live without measurement and comparison inwardly is only possible when you yourself are learning the whole implication of it – the aggression, the brutality, the division and its envies. Freedom means a life without comparison. But inevitably you will ask what is the condition of a life without any high or low, without an example, without division. You want a description of it so that through description you may capture it. This is another form of comparison and competition. The description is never the described. You have to live it and then you will know what it means.

5

Most of us do not seem to give sufficient importance to meditation. For most it is a passing thing in which some kind of experience is expected, some transcendental attainment, a fulfilment after all other attempts at fulfilment have failed. Meditation becomes a self-hypnotic movement in which appear various projections and symbols. But these are a continuity of what has been, perhaps modified or enlarged, but always within the area of some achievement. All this is rather immature and childish without great significance, and without breaking away from the established order – or disorder – of past events. These happenings become extraordinarily significant to a mind that is concerned with its own advancement, improvement and self-determined expectations. When the mind breaks through all this rubbish, which can only happen with self-knowing, then what happens can never be told to another. Even in the telling things have already changed. It is like describing a storm. It is already over the hills, the valleys, and gone beyond. And so the telling of it becomes something of the past and therefore no longer what is actually taking place. One can describe something accurately – an event – but the very accuracy of it becomes inaccurate when the thing has moved away. The accuracy of memory is a fact but memory is the result of something that has already happened. If the mind is following the flow of a river it has no time for description, nor for memory to gather itself. When this kind of meditation is going on a great many things take place which are not the projection of thought. Each event is totally new in the sense that memory cannot recognize it; and as it cannot recognize it, it cannot be gathered into words and memories. It is a thing that has never happened before. This is not an experience. Experience implies recognition, association and accumulation as knowledge. Obviously certain powers are released but these become a great danger as long as the self-centred activity goes on, whether these activities are identified with religious concepts or with personal tendencies.

Freedom from the self is absolutely necessary for the real thing to be. But thought is very cunning, extraordinarily subtle in its activities and unless one is tremendously aware, without any choice, of all these subtleties and cunning pursuits, meditation becomes the gaining of powers beyond the mere physical ones. Any sense of importance of any action of the self must lead inevitably to confusion and sorrow. That is why, before you consider meditation, begin with the understanding of yourself, the structure and the nature of thought. Otherwise you will get lost and your energies will be wasted. So to go far you must begin very near: and the first step is the last step.

The big room overlooked the blue Pacific. It was high on a cliff and from there you could see the waves breaking on the shore, white and spreading. It was very quiet though there were several young people there. We were all feeling rather shy. There were short-haired ones and long-haired, the bearded and the casual.

'First of all, if I may start out,' said a young man with clean long hair and beard, 'why should I earn my livelihood? Why should I make a career, knowing where it leads – property, bank account, a wife and children, and the utter middle-classness of it all? I don't want to be caught in that trap. If others want to, it is for them, but not for me. I don't mind being a beggar or asking people for a handout. I sleep in somebody's house and I have enough clothes to get along with. I have been all over the State for the past few years living this way and I like it. Let them all work if they wish and if they feel like supporting me – let them. I don't want to belong to any commune, to any group. I am free and I want to remain free. And I'm not against anyone – black or white. But I'm told this is exploitation: that while I'm young it is all right but when I'm in my thirties I'll begin to see I can't go on like this. I don't know what the future holds but I'm living from day to day and that's good enough. I would like your opinion on this.'

Only fools offer opinions. You know the monks in Asia live this way: not in organized communities but as individuals going from village to village begging and being protected. In return they preach the good life: not the physical good life but a life of goodness. That is what they offer, unless they are criminals or exploiters. So what are you offering in return to those who feed you?

'Why should I offer anything in return? I have nothing to give them. I don't want to tell them how to live. Any sensible man knows when the way he is living is bourgeois, square, and it is up to them to break away from it. I have tried talking to people but they don't care. I don't want to offer anything in return for their food and clothes. Basically I have nothing to offer. I don't paint, I don't play a guitar. I don't do any of the things they like. I am entirely outside their circle. If I had something basic I would offer it without caring whether they took it. But I've nothing. I am just as confused as the rest of the world and probably just as miserable. I'm not a drop-out. I've been through college and I'm disgusted with the whole thing; with their hypocrisies and with their pretensions. But what bothers me a little is, I want to find – not God, that is a bourgeois concept – but something that is real. I've read some Eastern books about this but they all take off on theories and ideas. I want to feel something real in my guts which they can't touch or take away. I want to get to the heart of it as quickly as possible. I see the absurdity of instant illumination but I haven't the patience to go through the rigmarole of discipline, fasting, following some system. I want to go straight to it on the shortest road possible.'

Surely this is possible: to see clearly 'what is' without any distortion, without any motive, and go beyond it. If you see

242

very clearly what is, you are already beyond it. And can you see very clearly what is? See not only the outward, the environment, the social morality, the bureaucratic sanctions, religious and worldly, but also inwardly? To see what is going on actually, without any choice, without any reservation. If you can, then the door is open. That is the shortest way and the most direct. Then you don't follow anybody. All systems are useless and the guru becomes a mischief-maker. Can you do this? If you can, then the mind is free and the heart is full. Then you are a light to yourself.

Another spoke. 'I am a drop-out. I dropped out of college. I took economics as my major and just before graduation I left. I saw what the professors were like, intriguing among themselves, playing politics for better positions. I saw their utter indifference to anything as long as they were secure in their professors' world. I didn't want to become like them. A few of us here in this room want to form a community. Most of us don't belong to anything. We have no sympathy with the battle that goes on between black and white; we welcome black and white, as you can see. We want to get a piece of land to live on, and we will. We can do things with our hands, we will cultivate it and sell things. But our question is, is it possible to live together without any conflict amongst ourselves, without any authority, and in great affection?'

A community is generally formed around an idea, a belief, or around someone who embodies that belief. The ideal or the Utopia becomes the authority and gradually some individual takes charge of it: guides, threatens and excommunicates. In this there is no co-operation at all; there is obedience which of course leads to disaster. Have you – if one may ask – considered this question of co-operation? If you have not, your community will inevitably fail. To live together and work together is one of the most difficult things. Each one wants to fulfil himself, become this or that, and therein lies the disruption of any co-operation. To work together implies the abnegation of the self without any motive. It is like learning together in which there is only function without any status. If you have this real understanding of the spirit of co-operation then it is bound to work. It isn't each one contributing something to the welfare of the community, but rather each one having this vital spark of understanding. Any personal motive or profit puts an end to the true quality of co-operation. Do you think that you and your friends have this? Or is it just that you want to start a community? That is like starting out on a boat, hoping to find an island, not knowing in what direction you are going, where you are going, but hoping to find somewhere somehow a happy land with a group of people who have no idea what to do with the land or themselves.

A young man with a sensitive face and hands said, 'I am one of those who take drugs. I've taken them regularly for four or five years; not too much; probably every month or so. I am well aware what it is doing to me. I am not quite as sharp as I was. When I'm high I think I can do anything. I seem to have tremendous energy and there is no confusion. I see things sharply. I feel like a god on earth, perfect, without any problems, without any regrets. But I can't maintain that state all the time and I'm back on this mad earth. Now I need a stronger dose and where it is leading me I really don't know. I'm uneasy about it now. I can see myself gradually ending up in a mental hospital, and yet the pull of the other state is so strong that I seem to have no resistance. I'm young. I'm not a drop-out. I live with my parents. They know what I'm doing and want to help me stop it. I see a slow deterioration in myself. I experimented with it in the beginning because the others did. It was fun then, but now it has become a danger. You see how clearly I can explain all this? But yet there is part of me that has become slow, lethargic and ineffectual. It is these drug-gurus that have hooked me on it, promising an experience that is the real thing. I see now how easily we are deceived by these intellectuals. I don't want to end up in a mental hospital or prison, or lose my mind altogether.'

If you see this so clearly, how it is damaging your brain and sensibilities and the subtleties of your life, why don't you drop it? Not for a day or two, but drop it completely? If you really see the danger of it, not verbally or romantically, the very seeing is the action that will put an end to it. But you must *see* it, not theorize about seeing. You must completely negate it. In this you will have the strength to do it, the vitality and energy. Then you will stop it without any resistance. It is this resistance that is the core of the matter. Don't build a resistance against it. Then you will be in conflict with the drug on one side and you on the other, with a wall of decision which only separates and increases conflict. Whereas if you really see it, see the tremendous danger of it as you would see the tremendous danger of a shark, or a rattlesnake, then you would drop it completely, instantly.

So, if we may suggest, don't decide not to take drugs, for decision is based on will, which is resistance with all its contradictions and conflicts. Being aware of this, you will then say it is impossible to give it up. Don't fight it but see actually the immense danger to the brain, to the whole nervous system, to the clarity of perception. That is all you have to do and nothing else: seeing is doing.

. 'May we all come back another day, Sir?'

Of course, as often as you like.

6

THERE IS NO sequence in meditation. There is no continuity for this implies time and space and action within that. Our whole psychological activity is within the field of time and space and from this follows action which is always incomplete. Our mind is conditioned to the acceptance of time and space. From here to there, the chain of this and that, is time-sequence. In this movement action will bring about contradiction and therefore conflict. This is our life. Can action ever be free of time, so that there are neither regrets nor anticipation, the backward and forward looking of action? Seeing is acting. It is not first understanding and then acting; but rather seeing which in itself is action. In this there is no element of time, so the mind is always free. Time and space are the way of thought which builds and nourishes the self, the me and the not-me, with all its demands for fulfilment, its resistance and fear of being hurt.

On this morning the quality of meditation was nothingness, the total emptiness of time and space. It is a fact and not an idea or the paradox of opposing speculations. One finds this strange emptiness when the root of all problems withers away. This root is thought, the thought that divides and holds. In meditation the mind actually becomes empty of the past, though it can use the past as thought. This goes on throughout the day and at night sleep is the emptiness of yesterday and therefore the mind touches that which is timeless.

The young man with the beard and very long hair said, 'I am an idealist who is a revolutionary. I don't want to wait for the slow progress of humanity. I want a radical change as quickly as possible. There are appalling social injustices among both blacks and whites, among all minorities, and of course the politicians, as they now are, are corrupt, self-seeking in the name of democracy, and hypocritical. I am violent by nature and I cannot see anyway except through violence to bring about a radical change in the social structure. I am an idealist in the sense that we will tear down the mess and let something new grow. The new is our ideal. I don't know what it will be, but as we destroy the old, we will find out. I know what you think of violence but this is neither here nor there. Most people in the world are already violent, full of antagonisms and we will use that to pull down the Establishment and make a new society. We are for freedom. We want to be free to express ourselves; each one must fulfil himself, and the present society denies all this. We are, of course, against all religions.'

The idealist who is also a revolutionary, though he may talk convincingly about freedom, inevitably will bring about a dictatorship of the few or of the many. He will also create a personal cult and destroy totally every form of freedom. You may have observed this in the French and Russian revolutions. Your ideal which may come out of the ashes of the present structure will only be speculative and theoretical and on this speculative Utopia – call it what you like – you want to build a new society. This is what all the physical revolutionaries have done. They start off with equality, social justice, the withering of the state and so on, and end up with a tyrannical bureaucracy, insistence on conformity and the exercise of authority in the name of the state. Surely this is not what you want. You feel or think that through the destruction of the present social structure, you will find as you go along, without having a blueprint, a new structure which you think will have social justice, freedom for all, economic equality and so on. You hope to produce all this through violence. Violence can only breed more violence. You may be able through violence to destroy present systems but it will breed resistance and deep-rooted unwillingness to co-operate.

It appears you all want quick changes only outwardly.

You want to end wars immediately, with which most of us agree, but as long as there are divisions of nationalities, of religious beliefs with their dogmas, there must be conflict. Any form of division will breed antagonism and hatred. We want to change the surface of things without going to the very heart of the matter. The heart of the matter is education. It is the total understanding of man and not an emphasis on one fragment of his life – whether it be technology or earning a livelihood.

We see that you are not listening to all this. If one may point it out, all the enthusiasts for outward change always brush aside the more fundamental issues.

'What you say may be so, but all that will take time and we haven't time now to be properly educated. We must change the structure first in order to have proper education.'

The postponement of fundamental questions makes for a greater superficiality of life, of everyday existence, and leads to various forms of escape, including violence – escapes through so-called religions, through entertainment. We are not dividing the outer and the inner. We are concerned with the total movement of life and education is part of this. As it is now, in almost every country there is some sort of military service. Instead of that it should be part of education to work in the social field. But this too is not the fundamental issue.

'You are not convincing me. You haven't shown me what to do and how to act in this murderous world.'

We are not trying to convince you of anything. We are pointing to certain facts, certain truths which are neither yours nor mine. We are saying that to bring about a radical change in the social structure, fundamental questions must be answered; and in the very asking is the answer. The answer is the action; not in some distant future, but now. That is the greatest revolution. The greatest and the only revolution. To that you reply: we haven't time, we want to change the social structure immediately. If we may point it out, this reply is utterly immature. Man is not merely a social machine. He is concerned with love, concerned with sex, with fears. Yet without taking all that into account, you hope by transforming the scaffolding of the social structure to bring about a radical change. The activist is the extrovert. But what we are concerned with is neither extrovert nor introvert – which again is a very superficial division. What really concerns us is the change of the human mind. If this is not deeply understood, your revolution will be a reform and like every reform will need further reform.

'I'm bored with all this.' A tall clean-shaven young man in sloppy clothes spoke. 'I'm not interested in this at all. But what does interest me – not as an escape – is really to find out what meditation is. Can we go into that?'

Sirs, you see how divided we all are. One occupied with your physical revolution, another with sex, another with art or writing, and another with the understanding of truth. All these fragmentations make man self-centred, confused and miserable. And you with your revolution hope to solve all these problems by changing the superficial structure. To that you will probably reply: change the environment and man will be different. But again that is only a partial answer, or the statement of a partial fact. We are concerned with the total understanding of man. And this is meditation. Meditation is not an escape from 'what is'. It is the understanding of it and going beyond it. Without understanding 'what is', meditation becomes merely a form of self-hypnosis and escape into visions and imaginative flights of fancy. Meditation is the understanding of the whole activity of thought which brings into being the 'me', the self, the ego, as a fact. Then thought tries to understand the image which it has created, as though that self were something permanent. This self again divides itself into the higher and the lower and this division in turn brings conflict, misery and confusion. The knowing of the self is one thing and the understanding of how the self comes into being, is another. One presupposes the existence of the self as a permanent entity. The other, through observation, learns how the self is put together by thought. So the understanding of thought, its ways and its subtleties, its activities and its divisions, is the beginning of meditation. But if you consider the self a permanent entity, you are studying a self which is non-existent, for it is merely a bundle of memories, words and experiences. So self-knowing is not the knowledge of the self but seeing how the self has been put together and how this makes for the fragmentation of life. One must see very clearly this misunderstanding. There is no permanent self about which to learn. But learning about the ways of thought and its activities is to dissipate self-centred activity. This is the foundation of meditation. Without understanding this deeply and radically, meditation becomes merely a game for the foolish, with their absurd little visions, fanciful experiences and the mischief of power. This foundation implies awareness, the observation of what is, without any choice, to see without any prejudice actually what is going on, both outwardly and inwardly, without any control or decision. This attention is action which is not something separate by itself; for life is action. You don't have to become an activist, which again is a fragmentation of life. If we are really concerned with total action, not a fragmentary one, then total action comes with total attention, which is to see actually 'what is' both inwardly and outwardly. And that very seeing is the doing.

'But don't you need training in this? Some method to practise so as to become attentive, so as to become sensitive?'

That is what so-called schools of meditation offer, which is really quite absurd. Method implies a mechanical repetition of words, or of control, or of conformity. In this repetition the mind becomes mechanical. A mind that is mechanical is not sensitive. In seeing the truth of this mechanical process the mind is liberated and therefore is sensitive. The seeing is the attention.

'But,' said the young man, 'I can't see clearly. How am I to do this?'

To see clearly there must be no choice, no prejudice, no

resistance or escape. Find out if you have escapes, if you are choosing, if you have prejudices. Understand this. Then the mind can observe very clearly not only the skies, the world, but what is going on within you – the self.

'But doesn't meditation bring about extraordinary experiences?'

Extraordinary experiences are totally irrelevant and dangerous. The mind being surfeited with experience wants wider, greater, more transcendent experience. The more is the enemy of the good. The good flowers only in the understanding of 'what is', not in wanting more or greater/experiences. In meditation there are certain things that do happen, for which there are no words; and if you talk about them, then they are not the real.

7

YOU LEAVE THE sea behind and go inland. This sea always seemed to be rough with huge waves. It is not blue but rather dark brown with strong currents. It looked like a dangerous sea. A river flowed into it in the rainy season, but after the monsoon the sea washed up so much sand that the little river was closed in. You left it and went inland passing many villages, bullock carts and three of the most sacred temples, and after a long while, crossing many hills you entered the valley and felt again its peculiar fascination.

The search for truth is such a false affair, as though by searching for it, asking others the way to it, reading about it in books, trying this or that system, you will be able to find it. To find it as if it were something there, fixed, motionless, and all you need do is recognize it, grasp it, and say you have found it.

It isn't far away: there is no path to it. It is not something you can capture, hold, treasure and verbally convey to another. Search implies a seeker and in that there is division, the everlasting fragmentation that man has made within himself and in all his activities. It is not that there must be an end to seeking but rather the beginning of learning. Learning is far more important than finding. To find one must have lost. Losing and recognizing is the pattern of search. One cannot experience truth. It does not give the satisfaction of achievement. It does not give one anything at all. It cannot be understood if the 'you' is still active.

No one can teach you about it so you need not follow anybody. All that one can do is to understand by careful observation the intricate movement of thought: how thought divides itself, how it creates its own opposites and thereby brings contradiction and conflict. Thought is so restless and in its restlessness it will attach itself to anything it thinks is essential, permanent, completely satisfying, and truth becomes its final attachment of satisfaction. You can never invite truth by any means. It is not an end; but it is there when the visual observation is very clear and when there is the perception of understanding. Understanding can take place only when there is complete freedom from all one's conditioning. It is this conditioning that is prejudice. So do not bother about truth but rather let the mind be aware of its own prison. Freedom is not in the prison. The beauty of emptiness is freedom.

On the same verandah, with the scent of the jasmine and the red flower of the tall tree, there was a group of boys and girls. They had shining faces and seemed extraordinarily cheerful. One of them asked, 'Sir, do you ever get hurt?'

You mean physically?

'Not quite, Sir. I don't know how to put it into words, but you feel inside that people can harm you, wound you, make you feel miserable. Someone says something and you shrink away. This is what I mean by hurt. We are all hurting each other in this way. Some do it deliberately, others without knowing it. Why do we get hurt? It is so unpleasant.'

Physical hurt is one thing and the other is much more complex. If you are physically hurt, you know what to do. You go to the doctor and he will do something about it. But if the memory of that hurt remains, then you are always nervous and apprehensive and this builds up a form of fear. There remains the memory of the past hurt which you don't want repeated. This is fairly understandable and can either become neurotic or be sanely dealt with without too much bother. But the other inward hurt needs very careful examination. One has to learn a great deal about it.

First of all, why do we get hurt at all? From childhood this seems to be a major factor in our lives: not to be hurt, not to be wounded by another, by a word, by a gesture, by a look, by any experience. Why do we get hurt? Is it because we are sensitive, or is it because we have an image of

ourselves which must be protected, which we feel is important for our very existence, an image without which we feel
lost, confused? There are these two things: the image and
sensitivity. Do you understand what we mean by being
sensitive, both physically and inwardly? If you are sensitive
and rather shy, you withdraw into yourself, build a wall
around yourself in order not to be hurt. You do this, don't
you? Once you have been hurt by a word or by a criticism,
and that has wounded you, you proceed to build a wall of
resistance. You don't want to be hurt any more. You may
have an image, an idea about yourself, that you are important, that you are clever, that your family is better than other
families, that you play games better than somebody else. You
have this image about yourself, don't you? And when the
importance of that image is questioned or shaken or broken
into fragments, you feel very hurt. There is self-pity, anxiety,
fear. And the next time you build a stronger image, more
affirmative, aggressive and so on. You see that nobody dis-
turbs you, which again is building a wall against any
encroachment. So the fact is that both the one who is sensitive and the image-maker bring about the walls of resistance.
Do you know what happens when you build a wall around
yourself? It is like building a very high wall around your
house. You don't see your neighbours, you don't get enough
sunlight, you live in a very small space with all the members
of your family. And not having enough space, you begin to
get on each other's nerves, you quarrel, become violent,
wanting to get away and revolt. And if you have enough
money and enough energy you build another house for yourself with another wall around it and so it goes on. Resistance
implies lack of space and it is one of the factors of violence.

'But,' asked one of them, 'mustn't one protect oneself?'

Against what? Naturally you must protect yourself
against disease, against the rains and the sun; but when you
say mustn't one protect oneself, are you not asking to build
a wall against being hurt? It may be your brother or your
mother against whom you build the wall, thinking to pro-

tect yourself, but ultimately this leads to your own destruction and the destruction of light and space.

'But,' asked one of the girls with studious eyes and long plaited hair, 'what am I to do when I am hurt? I know I'm hurt. I get hurt so often. What am I to do? You say I mustn't build a wall of resistance but I can't live with so many wounds.'

Do you understand, if one may ask, why you are hurt? And also when you get hurt? Do look at that leaf or that flower. It is very delicate and the beauty of it is in its very delicacy. It is terribly vulnerable and yet it lives. And you who so often are wounded, have you asked when and why you get hurt? Why do you get hurt – when somebody says something you don't like, when somebody is aggressive, violent towards you. Then why are you hurt? If you get hurt and build a wall around yourself, which is to withdraw, then you live in a very small space within yourself. In that small space there is no light or freedom and you will get more and more hurt. So the question is, can you live freely and happily without being hurt, without building walls of resistance. This is the important question, isn't it? Not how to strengthen the walls or what to do when you have a wall round your little space. So there are two things involved in this: the memory of the hurt and the prevention of future hurts. If that memory continues and you add to it fresh memories of hurts, then your wall becomes stronger and higher, the space and the light become smaller and duller, and there is great misery, mounting self-pity and bitterness. If you see very clearly the danger of it, the uselessness, the pity of it, then the past memories will wither away. But you must see it as you would see the danger of a cobra. Then you know it is a deadly danger and you go nowhere near it. In the same way do you see the danger of past memories with their hurts, with their walls of self-defence? Do you actually see it as you see that flower? If you do then it inevitably disappears.

So you know what to do with past hurts. Then how will

you prevent future hurts? Not by building walls. That is clear, isn't it? If you do, you will get more and more hurt. Please listen to this question carefully. Knowing that you may be hurt, how will you prevent this hurt taking place? If somebody tells you that you are not clever or beautiful, you get hurt, or angry, which is another form of resistance. Now what can you do? You saw very clearly how the past hurts go away without any effort; you saw because you listened and gave your attention. Now when someone says something unpleasant to you, be attentive; listen very carefully. Attention will prevent the mark of hurt. Do you understand what we mean by attention?

'You mean, Sir, concentration, don't you?'

Not quite. Concentration is a form of resistance, is a form of exclusion, a shutting out, a retreat. But attention is something quite different. In concentration there is a centre from which the action of observation takes place. Where there is a centre, the radius of its observation is very limited. Where there is no centre, observation is vast, clear. This is attention.

'I'm afraid we don't understand this at all, Sir.'

Look out at those hills, see the light on them, see those trees, hear the bullock cart going by; see the yellow leaves, the dried river bed, and that crow sitting on the branch. Look at all of this. If you look from a centre, with its prejudice, with its fear, with its like and dislike, then you don't see the vast expanse of this earth. Then your eyes are clouded, then you become myopic and your eyesight becomes twisted. Can you look at all this, the beauty of the valley, the sky, without a centre? Then that is attention. Then listen with attention and without the centre, to another's criticism, insult, anger, prejudice. Because there is no centre in that attention there is no possibility of being hurt. But where there is a centre there is inevitable hurt. Then life becomes one scream of fear.

8

MEDITATION IS NEVER the control of the body. There is no actual division between the organism and the mind. The brain, the nervous system and the thing we call the mind are all one, indivisible. It is the natural act of meditation that brings about the harmonious movement of the whole. To divide the body from the mind and to control the body with intellectual decisions is to bring about contradiction, from which arise various forms of struggle, conflict and resistance.

Every decision to control only breeds resistance, even the determination to be aware. Meditation is the understanding of the division brought about by decision. Freedom is not the act of decision but the act of perception. The seeing is the doing. It is not a determination to see and then to act. After all, will is desire with all its contradictions. When one desire assumes authority over another, that desire becomes will. In this there is inevitable division. And meditation is the understanding of desire, not the overcoming of one desire by another. Desire is the movement of sensation, which becomes pleasure and fear. This is sustained by the constant dwelling of thought upon one or the other. Meditation really is a complete emptying of the mind. Then there is only the functioning of the body; there is only the activity of the organism and nothing else; then thought functions without identification as the me and the not-me. Thought is mechanical, as is the organism. What creates conflict is thought identifying itself with one of its parts which becomes the me, the self and the various divisions in that self. There is no need for the self at any time. There is nothing but the body and freedom of the mind can happen only when thought is not breeding the me. There is no self to understand but only the thought that creates the self. When there is only the organism without the self, perception, both visual and non-visual, can never be distorted. There is only seeing 'what is' and that very perception goes beyond what is. The emptying of the mind is not an activity of thought or an intellectual process. The continuous seeing of what is without any kind of distortion naturally empties the mind of all thought and yet that very mind can use thought when it is necessary. Thought is mechanical and meditation is not.

It was very early and in the morning light two owls were sitting in the tamarind tree. They were small ones and always seemed to go in pairs. They had been crying all night, off and on, and one came to the window-sill and called to the other with a rattling note. The two on the branch had their hole in the tree. They were often there in the morning before they retired for the day, sitting there very grey and silent. Presently one would gently withdraw and disappear into the hole and the other would follow, but they made no noise. They only talked and rattled in the night. The tamarind tree not only sheltered the owls but also many parrots. It was a huge tree in the garden overlooking the river. There were vultures, crows and the green-golden flycatchers. The flycatchers would often come to the window-sill on the verandah, but you have to sit very still and not even move your eyes. They had a curious curving flight and they kept to themselves, unlike the crows that pestered the vultures. There were monkeys too that morning. They had been there in the distance but now they had all come closer to the house. They remained for a few days and after they left there was a lonely male who appeared every morning on the tallest of the tamarinds. He would climb to the highest branch and sit there looking at the river, at the villagers passing by and the cattle grazing. As the sun grew warmer, he would climb down slowly and disappear, and the next morning he would again be there as the sun came over the trees, making a golden path on the river. For two whole weeks he was there, lonely, aloof, watching. He had no companion and one morning he disappeared.

The students had returned. One of the boys asked, 'Mustn't one obey one's parents? After all, they brought me up, they are educating me. Without money I couldn't come to this school, so they are responsible for me and I am responsible to them. It is this feeling of responsibility that makes me feel I must obey them. After all, they may know much better than I do what is good for me. They want me to be an engineer.'

Do you want to be an engineer? Or are you merely studying engineering because your parents want it?

'I don't know what I want to do. Most of us in this room don't know what we want to do. We have government scholarships. We can take any subject we like but our parents and society say that engineering is a good profession. They need engineers. But when you ask us what we want to do we become rather uncertain and this is confusing and disturbing.'

You said that your parents are responsible for you and that you must obey them. You know what is happening in the West where there is no parental authority any more. There the young people don't want any authority, though they have their own peculiar kind. Does responsibility demand authority, obedience, accepting the wishes of parents or the demands of society? Doesn't responsibility mean having the capacity for rational conduct? Your parents think that you are not capable of this and so they feel called upon to watch over your behaviour, what you do, what you study and what you might become. Their idea of moral conduct is based upon their conditioning, upon their education, upon their beliefs, fears and pleasures. The past generation has built a social structure and they want you to conform to that structure. They think it is moral and they feel they know much more than you do. And you in your turn, if you conform will see that your children also conform. So gradually the authority of conformity becomes moral excellence. Is that what you are asking when you wonder if you should obey your parents?

You see what this obeying means? When you are very young you hear what your parents tell you. The constant repetition of your hearing what they say establishes the act of obedience. So obedience becomes mechanical. It is like a soldier who hears an order over and over again and complies, becomes subservient. And that is how most of us live. That is propaganda, both religious and worldly. So you see, a habit has been formed from childhood of hearing what your parents have told you, of what you have read. So hearing becomes the means of obedience. And now you are faced with the problem of whether you should obey or not obey: obey what others have said or obey your own urges. You want to hear what your desires say and that very hearing will make you obey your desires. Out of this arises opposition and resistance. So when you ask whether you should obey your parents there is a fear that if you didn't obey you might go wrong and that they might not give you money to be educated. In obedience there is always fear, and fear darkens the mind.

So instead of asking that question, find out if you can talk to your parents rationally and also find out what it means to hear. Can you hear without any fear what they say? And can you also listen to your own urges and desires without fear of going wrong? If you can listen quietly without fear you will find out for yourself whether you should obey, not only your parents, but every form of authority. You see, we have been educated in a most absurd way. We have never been taught the act of learning. A lot of information is poured into our heads and we develop a very small part of the brain which will help us to earn a livelihood. The rest of the brain is neglected. It is like the cultivation of a corner in a vast field and the rest of the field stays overgrown with weeds, thistles and thorns.

So now, how are you listening or hearing what we are saying? Will this hearing make you obey or will it make you intelligent, aware not only of the small corner but of the whole vast field? Neither your teachers nor your parents are concerned with the greatness of the field with all its content. But they are intensely, insanely concerned with the corner. The corner seems to give security and that is their concern. You may revolt against it – and people are doing this – but again those in revolt are concerned only with their piece of the corner. And so it goes on. So can you hear without obedience, without following? If you can, there will be sensitivity and concern for the whole field and this concern brings about intelligence. It is this intelligence which will act instead of the mechanical habit of obedience.

'Oh,' said a girl, 'but our parents love us. They don't want any harm for us. It is out of love they want us to obey, tell us what studies we must take, how to shape our lives.'

Every parent says he loves his children. It is only the abnormal who hates his children or the abnormal child that really hates his parents. Every parent throughout the world says he loves his children, but does he? Love implies care, great concern not only when they are young, but to see that they have the right kind of education, that they are not killed in wars, and to see to a change in the social structure with its absurd morality. If the parents have love for their children they will see that they do not conform; they will see that they learn instead of imitate. If they really love them they will bring about vast changes so that you can live sanely, happily and securely. Not only you in this room but everyone all over the world. Love doesn't demand conformity. Love offers freedom. Not what you want to do, which is generally very shallow, petty and mean, but to understand, to listen freely, to listen without the poison of conformity. Do you think if parents really loved, that there would be war? From childhood you are taught to dislike your neighbour, told you are different from somebody else. You are brought up in prejudice so that when you grow up you become violent, aggressive, self-centred, and the whole cycle is repeated over again. So learn what it means to hear;

learn to listen freely without accepting or denying, without conformity or resistance. Then you will know what to do. Then you will find out what goodness is and how it flowers. And it will never flower in any corner: it flowers only in the vast field of life, in the action of the whole field.